W9-BKC-614

one pot

& slow cooking

essential recipes

Publisher's Note:
Raw or semi-cooked eggs should not be consumed by babies, toddlers, pregnant or breast-feeding women, the elderly or those suffering from a chronic illness.

Recipe Note:
All eggs are large size and all vegetables are medium size, unless otherwise stated.

Publisher and Creative Director: Nick Wells
Project Editor: Catherine Taylor
Copy Editor: Kathy Steer
Photographers: Colin Bowling, Paul Forrester and Stephen Brayne
Home Economists & Stylists: Ann Nicol, Jaqueline Bellefontaine, Mandy Phipps, Vicki Smallwood and Penny Stephens
Art Director: Mike Spender
Layout Design: Dave Jones
Digital Design and Production: Chris Herbert and Claire Walker
Proofreader: Dawn Laker

Special thanks to: Joseph Kelly.

11 13 15 14 12

1 3 5 7 9 10 8 6 4 2

This edition first published 2011 by
FLAME TREE PUBLISHING
Crabtree Hall, Crabtree Lane
Fulham, London SW6 6TY
United Kingdom

www.flametreepublishing.com

Flame Tree is part of The Foundry Creative Media Co. Ltd

© 2011 this edition The Foundry Creative Media Co. Ltd

ISBN 978-0-85775-153-9

A CIP record for this book is available from the British Library upon request.

Printed in China

one pot

& slow cooking

essential recipes

General Editor: Gina Steer

FLAME TREE
PUBLISHING

Contents

Fish & Seafood 128

Vegetables 170

Hygiene in the Kitchen

It is important to remember that many foods can carry some form of bacteria. In most cases, the worst it will lead to is a bout of food poisoning or gastroenteritis, but this can be serious for certain people. The risk can be reduced or eliminated, however, by good hygiene and proper cooking.

Do not buy food that is past its sell, or pull, date and do not consume food past its expiration date. When buying food, use your eyes and nose. If the food looks tired, limp, or a bad color or it has a rank, acrid, or bad smell, do not buy or eat it under any circumstances.

Dish towels must be washed and changed regularly. Ideally, use disposable cloths, which should be replaced on a daily basis. More durable cloths should be left to soak in bleach, then washed in the washing machine at a high temperature. Keep your hands, cooking utensils, and food preparation surfaces clean and do not let pets climb onto any work counters. Avoid handling food if you have a stomach ache because bacteria can be passed on through food preparation.

Buying

Avoid bulk buying where possible, especially fresh produce. Fresh foods lose their nutritional value rapidly, so buying a little at a time minimizes loss of nutrients. Check that any packaging is intact and not damaged or pierced. Store fresh foods in the refrigerator as soon as possible.

When buying frozen foods, make sure that they are not heavily iced on the outside and that the contents feel completely frozen. Make sure that they have been stored in the cabinet at the correct storage level and the temperature is below -0.4˚F. Pack in cooler bags to transport home and place in the freezer as soon as possible after purchase.

Preparation

Be especially careful when preparing raw meat and fish. A separate cutting board should be used for each, and the knife, board, and your hands should be thoroughly washed before handling or preparing any other food. A variety of good-quality plastic boards come in various designs and colors. This makes differentiating easier and the plastic has the added hygienic advantage of being washable at high temperatures in the dishwasher. If using the board for fish, first wash in cold water, then in hot to prevent odor.

When cooking, be particularly careful to keep cooked and raw food separate to avoid cross-contamination. It is worth washing all fruits and vegetables regardless of whether they are going to be eaten raw or lightly cooked. This rule should apply even to packages of prewashed herbs and salads.

Do not reheat food more than once. If using a microwave, always check that the food is piping hot all the way through—in theory, the food should reach 158˚F and needs to be cooked at that temperature for at least 3 minutes to make sure that all bacteria are killed.

All poultry must be thoroughly thawed before using. Remove the food to be thawed from the freezer and place in a shallow dish to contain the juices. Leave the food in the refrigerator until it is completely thawed. A 3-pound whole chicken will take about 26–30 hours to thaw. To speed up the process, immerse the chicken in cold water, making sure that the water is changed regularly. When the pieces can move freely and no ice crystals remain in the cavity, the bird is completely thawed. Once thawed, remove the packaging and pat the chicken dry. Place the chicken in a shallow dish, cover lightly, and store as close to the bottom of the refrigerator as possible. The chicken should be cooked as soon as possible.

Some foods can be cooked from frozen, including many prepared foods, such as soups, sauces, casseroles, and breads. Where applicable, follow the manufacturers' directions. Vegetables and fruits can also be cooked from frozen, but meats and fish should be thawed first. The only time food can be refrozen is when the food has been thoroughly thawed, then cooked. Once the food has cooled, then it can be frozen again, but it should only be stored for one month.

All poultry and game (except for duck) must be cooked thoroughly. When cooked, the juices will run clear on the thickest part of the bird—the best area to try is usually the thigh. Other meats, such as ground meat and pork, should be cooked all the way through. Fish should turn opaque, be firm in texture, and break easily into large flakes.

When cooking leftovers, make sure they are reheated until piping hot and that any sauce or soup reaches boiling point first.

Storing, Refrigerating, and Freezing

Meat, poultry, fish, seafood, and dairy products should all be refrigerated. The temperature of the refrigerator should be between 34°F and 41°F, while the freezer temperature should not rise above -0.4°F. To ensure the optimum temperature, avoid leaving the door open for long periods. Try not to overstock, because this reduces the airflow inside and, therefore, the effectiveness in cooling the food within.

When refrigerating cooked food, let it cool down completely before refrigerating. Hot food will raise the temperature of the refrigerator and possibly affect or spoil other food stored in it.

Food should always be covered. Raw and cooked food should be stored in separate parts of the refrigerator. Cooked food should be kept on the top shelves, while raw meat, poultry, and fish should be placed on the bottom to avoid drips and cross-contamination. It is recommended that eggs be refrigerated in order to maintain their freshness and shelf life.

Regularly clean, defrost, and clear out the refrigerator or freezer—it is worth checking the packaging to see exactly how long each product is safe to freeze. Be careful that frozen foods are not kept stored in the freezer for too long.

Blanched vegetables can be stored for one month; beef, lamb, poultry, and pork for six months; and unblanched vegetables and fruits in syrup for a year. Oily fish and sausages can be stored for three months. Dairy products can last four to six months, while cakes and pastries can be kept in the freezer for three to six months.

High-Risk Foods

Certain foods carry risks to people who are considered vulnerable, such as the elderly, the ill, pregnant women, babies, young infants, and those people with a chronic illness.

There is a slight chance that some eggs carry the bacteria salmonella. Cook the eggs until both the yolk and the white are firm to eliminate this risk. Pay particular attention to dishes and products incorporating lightly cooked or raw eggs, which should be eliminated from the diet. Hollandaise sauce, mayonnaise, mousses, soufflés, and meringues all use raw or lightly cooked eggs, as do custard-based dishes, ice creams, and sorbets. These are all considered high-risk foods to the vulnerable groups mentioned above.

Certain meats and poultry also carry the potential risk of salmonella and so should be cooked thoroughly until the juices run clear and there is no pinkness left. Unpasteurized products, such as milk, cheese (especially soft cheese), pâté, and meat (both raw and cooked), all have the potential risk of listeria and should be avoided.

When buying seafood, buy from a reputable source that has a high turnover to ensure freshness. Fish should have bright, clear eyes, shiny skin, and bright pink or red gills. The fish should feel stiff to the touch, with a slight smell of sea air. The flesh of fish steaks and fillets should be translucent with no signs of discoloration. Mollusks, such as scallops, clams, and mussels, are sold fresh and are still alive. Avoid any that are open or do not close when tapped lightly. In the same way, univalves, such as abalones or periwinkles, should withdraw back into their shells when lightly prodded. When choosing cephalopods, such as squid and octopus, they should have a firm flesh and pleasant sea smell. With all seafood, care is required when freezing it. If it has been frozen, it should not be frozen again under any circumstances.

Nutrition: The Role of Essential Nutrients

A healthy and well-balanced diet is the body's primary energy source. In children, it constitutes the building blocks for future health as well as providing a lot of energy. In adults, it encourages self-healing and regeneration within the body. A well-balanced diet will provide the body with all the essential nutrients it needs. This can be achieved by eating a variety of foods, demonstrated in the pyramid below.

FATS

PROTEINS

milk, yogurt, and cheese   meat, fish, poultry, eggs, nuts, and beans

FRUIT AND VEGETABLES

STARCHY CARBOHYDRATES

cereals, potatoes, bread, rice, and pasta

FATS

Fats fall into two categories: saturated and unsaturated. Fats are an essential part of the diet; they are a source of energy and provide essential fatty acids and fat-soluble vitamins, but it is very important that a healthy balance is achieved. The right balance should boost the body's immunity to infection and keep muscles, nerves, and arteries in good condition. Saturated fats are of animal origin and can be found in dairy produce, meat, eggs, margarines, and hard, white cooking fat (lard) as well as in manufactured products, such as pies, cookies, and cakes. A high intake of saturated fat over many years has been proven to increase heart disease and high blood cholesterol levels and often leads to weight gain. Lowering the amount of saturated fat that we consume is very important, but this does not mean that it is good to consume a lot of other types of fat.

There are two kinds of unsaturated fats: polyunsaturated and monounsaturated. Polyunsaturated fats include safflower, soybean, corn, and sesame oils. The Omega-3 oils in polyunsaturated fats have been found to be beneficial to coronary health and can encourage brain growth and development. They are derived from oily fish, such as salmon, mackerel, herring, pilchards, and sardines. It is recommended that we should eat these types of fish at least once a week. Alternative liver oil supplements are also available. The most popular oils that are high in monounsaturates are olive oil, sunflower oil, and peanut oil. Monounsaturated fats are also known to help reduce the levels of cholestrol.

PROTEINS

Composed of amino acids—proteins' building blocks—proteins perform a wide variety of essential functions for the body, including supplying energy and building and repairing tissues. Good sources of proteins are eggs, milk, yogurt, cheese, meat, fish, poultry, nuts, and beans. (See the second level of the pyramid.) Some of these foods, however, contain saturated fats. To strike a nutritional balance, eat generous amounts of vegetable protein foods, such as soybeans and other beans, lentils, peas, and nuts.

MINERALS

CALCIUM Important for healthy bones and teeth, nerve transmission, muscle contraction, blood clotting, and hormone function. Calcium promotes a healthy heart, improves skin, relieves aching muscles and bones, maintains the correct acid-alkaline balance, and reduces menstrual cramps. Good sources are dairy products, small bones of small fish, nuts, beans, fortified white flours, breads, and green leafy vegetables.

CHROMIUM Balances blood sugar levels, helps to normalize hunger and reduce cravings, improves lifespan, helps protect DNA, and is essential for heart function. Good sources are brewer's yeast, whole-wheat bread, rye bread, oysters, potatoes, green bell peppers, butter, and parsnips.

IODINE Important for the manufacture of thyroid hormones and for normal development. Good sources are seafood, seaweed, milk, and dairy.

IRON As a component of hemoglobin, iron carries oxygen around the body. It is vital for normal growth and development. Good sources are liver, corned beef, red meat, fortified breakfast cereals, beans, green leafy vegetables, egg yolk, and cocoa and cocoa products.

MAGNESIUM Important for efficient functioning of metabolic enzymes and development of the skeleton. Magnesium promotes healthy muscles by helping them to relax and is, therefore, good for PMS. It is also important for heart muscles and the nervous system. Good sources are nuts, green vegetables, meat, cereals, milk, and yogurt.

PHOSPHORUS Forms and maintains bones and teeth, builds muscle tissue, helps maintain pH of the body, and aids metabolism and energy production. Phosphorus is present in almost all foods.

POTASSIUM Enables processing of nutrients; promotes healthy nerves and muscles; maintains fluid balance; helps secretion of insulin for blood sugar control; relaxes muscles; maintains heart functioning; and stimulates digestive movement. Good sources are fruit, vegetables, milk, and bread.

SELENIUM Antioxidant properties help to protect against free radicals and carcinogens. Selenium reduces inflammation, stimulates the immune system, promotes a healthy heart, and helps vitamin E's action. Necessary for the male reproductive system and for metabolism. Good sources are tuna, liver, kidney, meat, eggs, cereals, nuts, and dairy products.

SODIUM Important in helping to control body fluid, preventing dehydration. Sodium is involved in muscle and nerve function and helps move nutrients into cells. All foods are good sources. Processed, pickled, and salted foods are richest in sodium, but should be eaten in moderation.

ZINC Important for metabolism and healing; aids ability to cope with stress; promotes a healthy nervous system and brain, especially in the growing fetus; aids bone and tooth formation; and is essential for energy. Good sources are liver, meat, beans, whole-grain cereals, nuts, and oysters.

VITAMINS

VITAMIN A Important for cell growth and development and for the formation of visual pigments in the eye. Vitamin A comes in two forms: retinol and beta-carotene. Retinol is found in liver, meat, and whole milk. Beta-carotene is a powerful antioxidant and is found in red and yellow fruits and vegetables, such as carrots, mangoes, and apricots.

VITAMIN B1 (THIAMINE) Important in releasing energy from carbohydrate-containing foods. Good sources are yeast and yeast products, bread, fortified breakfast cereals, and potatoes.

VITAMIN B2 (RIBOFLAVIN) Important for metabolism of proteins, fats, and carbohydrates to produce energy. Good sources are meat, yeast extracts, fortified breakfast cereals, and milk and its products.

VITAMIN B3 (NIACIN) Required for the metabolism of food into energy. Good sources are milk, fortified cereals, beans, meat, poultry, and eggs.

VITAMIN B5 (PANTOTHENIC ACID) Important for the metabolism of food and energy production. All foods are good sources, but especially fortified breakfast cereals, wholegrain bread, and dairy products.

VITAMIN B6 Important for metabolism of protein and fat. Vitamin B6 may also be involved in the regulation of sex hormones. Good sources are liver, fish, pork, soybeans, and peanuts.

VITAMIN B7 (BIOTIN) Important for metabolism of fatty acids. Good sources are liver, kidney, eggs, and nuts.

VITAMIN B9 (FOLIC ACID) Critical during pregnancy for brain and nerve development. It is always essential for brain and nerve function, for utilizing protein, and for red blood cell formation. Good sources are whole-grain and fortified cereals, green leafy vegetables, oranges, and liver.

VITAMIN B12 Important for the production of red blood cells and DNA. It is vital for growth and the nervous system. Good sources are meat, fish, eggs, poultry, and milk.

VITAMIN C Important for healing wounds and the formation of collagen, which keeps skin and bones strong. It is an important antioxidant. Good sources are fruits, especially berries, and vegetables.

VITAMIN D Important for absorption and handling of calcium to help build bone strength. Good sources are oily fish, eggs, whole milk and milk products, margarine, and, of course, sufficient exposure to sunlight, because vitamin D is made in the skin.

VITAMIN E Important as an antioxidant vitamin helping to protect cell membranes from damage. Good sources are vegetable oils, margarines, seeds, nuts, and green vegetables.

VITAMIN K Important for controlling blood clotting. Good sources are cauliflower, Brussels sprouts, lettuce, cabbage, beans, broccoli, peas, asparagus, potatoes, corn oil, tomatoes, and milk.

CARBOHYDRATES

Carbohydrates are an energy source and come in two forms: starch and sugar. Starch carbohydrates are also known as complex carbohydrates and they include all cereals, potatoes, breads, rice, and pasta. Eating whole-grain varieties of these foods also provides fiber. Diets high in fiber are believed to be beneficial in helping to prevent bowel cancer and keep cholesterol down. Sugar carbohydrates—also known as fast-release carbohydrates because they provide a quick fix of energy—include sugar and sugar-sweetened products. Other sugars are lactose (from milk) and fructose (from fruit).

Meat

Looking to fill your home with the savory smells of an old-fashioned, hearty meal? Beef Bourguignon and Chili Con Carne are must tries. Or Pork with Tofu & Coconut could be a refreshing idea. If you have cast-iron cookware that can be used on the stove as well as in the oven, then you will truly be 'one pot' cooking; if not, use a pan on the stove and then transfer to an ovenproof casserole dish to get the 'slow-cooked' style.

Vietnamese Beef & Rice Noodle Soup

1 Place all the ingredients for the beef stock into a large stockpot or saucepan and cover with cold water. Bring to a boil and skim off any scum that rises to the surface. Reduce the heat and simmer gently, partially covered, for 2–3 hours, skimming occasionally.

2 Strain into a large bowl and let cool, then skim off the fat. Chill in the refrigerator, and, when cold, remove any fat from the surface. Pour 6 cups of the stock into a large wok and set aside.

3 Cover the noodles with warm water and leave for 3 minutes, or until just softened. Drain, then cut into 4-inch lengths.

4 Arrange the scallions and chile on a serving platter or large serving plate. Strip the leaves from the cilantro and mint, and then arrange them in piles on the plate.

5 Bring the stock in the wok to a boil over high heat. Add the noodles and simmer for about 2 minutes until tender. Add the beef strips and simmer for about 1 minute. Season to taste with salt and pepper. Ladle the soup with the noodles and beef strips into individual soup bowls, and serve immediately, with the plate of condiments handed around separately.

Ingredients   SERVES 4–6

For the beef stock:
2 lb. meaty beef bones
1 large onion, peeled and quartered
2 carrots, peeled and cut into chunks
2 celery stalks, trimmed and sliced
1 leek, washed and sliced into chunks
2 garlic cloves, unpeeled and
   lightly crushed
3 whole star anise
1 tsp. black peppercorns

For the soup:
$2^1/_2$ cups dried rice
   stick noodles
4–6 scallions, trimmed and
   diagonally sliced
1 red chile, seeded and
   diagonally sliced
1 small bunch fresh cilantro
1 small bunch fresh mint
$3/_4$ lb. beef tenderloin, very
   thinly sliced
salt and freshly ground black pepper

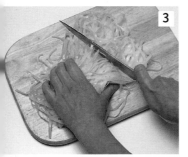

Chinese Cabbage & Mushroom Soup

1 Trim the stem ends of the Chinese cabbage and cut in half lengthwise. Remove the triangular core, then cut into 1-inch slices and set aside.

2 Place the dried shiitake mushrooms in a bowl and add enough almost-boiling water to cover. Let stand for 20 minutes to soften, then gently lift out and squeeze out the liquid. Discard the stems and thinly slice the caps, and set aside. Strain the liquid through a cheesecloth-lined strainer and set aside.

3 Heat a wok over medium-high heat, add the oil, and, when hot, add the bacon. Stir-fry for 3–4 minutes until crisp and golden, stirring frequently. Add the ginger and cremini mushrooms, and stir-fry for an additional 2–3 minutes.

4 Add the chicken stock and bring to a boil, skimming any fat and scum that rises to the surface. Add the scallions, sherry or rice wine, Chinese cabbage, and sliced mushrooms, and season to taste with salt and pepper. Pour in the soaking liquid and reduce the heat to the lowest possible setting.

5 Simmer gently, covered, until all the vegetables are tender; this will take about 10 minutes. Add a little water if the liquid has reduced too much. Spoon into soup bowls and drizzle with a little sesame oil. Serve immediately.

Ingredients   SERVES 4–6

1 lb. Chinese cabbage

$^1/_4$ cup dried shiitake mushrooms

1 tbsp. vegetable oil

3 oz. diced bacon

1-in. piece fresh ginger, peeled and finely chopped

$1^1/_2$ cups thinly sliced cremini mushrooms

5 cups chicken stock

4–6 scallions, trimmed and cut into short lengths

2 tbsp. dry sherry or Chinese rice wine

salt and freshly ground black pepper

sesame oil, for drizzling

Tasty tip
If Chinese leaves are not available, use Savoy cabbage.

Classic Minestrone

1 Heat the butter and olive oil together in a large saucepan. Chop the bacon and add to the saucepan. Cook for 3–4 minutes, then remove with a slotted spoon and set aside.

2 Finely chop the onion, garlic, celery, and carrots, and add to the saucepan, one ingredient at a time, stirring well after each addition. Cover and cook gently for 8–10 minutes until the vegetables are softened.

3 Add the chopped tomatoes with their juice and the stock, bring to a boil, then cover the saucepan with a lid, reduce the heat, and simmer gently for about 20 minutes.

4 Stir in the cabbage, beans, peas, and spaghetti. Cover and simmer for an additional 20 minutes, or until all the ingredients are tender. Season to taste with salt and pepper.

5 Return the cooked bacon to the saucepan and bring the soup to a boil. Serve the soup immediately with Parmesan cheese shavings sprinkled on the top and plenty of crusty bread.

Ingredients   SERVES 6–8

2 tbsp. butter
3 tbsp. olive oil
3 slices bacon
1 large onion, peeled
1 garlic clove, peeled
1 celery stalk, trimmed
2 carrots, peeled
14 oz. canned chopped tomatoes
5 cups chicken stock
$1^{1}/_{2}$ cups finely shredded
   green cabbage
$^{1}/_{2}$ cup trimmed and halved
   green beans
3 tbsp. frozen peas
$^{3}/_{4}$ cup spaghetti, broken into
   short pieces
salt and freshly ground black pepper
Parmesan cheese, to garnish
crusty bread, to serve

Beef Bourguignon

1 Preheat the oven to 325°F. Cut the beef and pork into small pieces and set aside. Heat 1 tablespoon of the oil in a flameproof casserole dish (or skillet, if preferred), add the meat, and cook in batches for 5–8 minutes until sealed. Remove with a slotted spoon and set aside.

2 Add the remaining oil to the casserole dish, then add the shallots, carrots, and garlic, and cook for 10 minutes. Return the meat to the casserole dish and sprinkle in the flour. Cook for 2 minutes, stirring occasionally, before pouring in the brandy, if using. Heat for 1 minute, then take off the heat and, if using the brandy, ignite and wait for the flames to subside before the next step.

3 Pour in the wine and stock. Return to the heat and bring to a boil, stirring continuously.

4 If a skillet has been used, transfer everything to an ovenproof dish. Add the bay leaf and season to taste with salt and pepper. Cover with a lid and cook in the oven for 1 hour.

5 Cut the potatoes in half. Remove the casserole dish from the oven and add the potatoes. Cook for an additional 1 hour, or until the meat and potatoes are tender. Serve sprinkled with chopped parsley.

Ingredients SERVES 4

$1^1/_2$ lb. braising beef, trimmed
8 oz. pork belly or lardons
2 tbsp. olive oil
12 shallots, peeled
$1^3/_4$ cups sliced carrots
2 garlic cloves, peeled
    and sliced
2 tbsp. all-purpose flour
3 tbsp. brandy (optional)
scant $^2/_3$ cup red wine, such as
    a Burgundy
2 cups beef stock
1 bay leaf
salt and freshly ground black pepper
1 lb. new potatoes, scrubbed
1 tbsp. freshly chopped parsley,
    to garnish

Tasty tip
If time allows, increase the wine to 1 cup and marinate the beef in the refrigerator overnight.

Steak & Kidney Stew

1 Heat the oil in a large, heavy saucepan, add the onion, garlic, and celery, and sauté for 5 minutes, or until browned. Remove from the pan with a slotted spoon and set aside.

2 Add the steak and kidneys to the pan and cook for 3–5 minutes until sealed, then return the onion mixture to the pan. Sprinkle in the flour and cook, stirring, for 2 minutes. Take off the heat, stir in the tomato paste, then the stock, and season to taste with salt and pepper. Add the bay leaf.

3 Return to the heat and bring to a boil, stirring occasionally. Add the carrots, then reduce the heat to a simmer and cover with a lid. Cook for 1¼ hours, stirring occasionally. Reduce the heat if the liquid is evaporating quickly. Add the potatoes and cook for another 30 minutes.

4 Place the flour, suet or shortening, and herbs in a bowl, and add a little seasoning. Add the water and mix to a stiff mixture. Using a little extra flour, shape into 8 small balls. Place the dumplings on top of the stew, cover with the lid, and continue to cook for 15 minutes, or until the meat is tender and the dumplings are well risen and fluffy. Stir in the spinach and let stand for 2 minutes, or until the spinach has wilted, then serve.

Ingredients — SERVES 4

1 tbsp. olive oil
1 onion, peeled and chopped
2–3 garlic cloves, peeled and crushed
2 celery stalks, trimmed and sliced
1¼ lb. braising beef, trimmed
   and diced
4 oz. lamb kidneys, cored
   and chopped
2 tbsp. all-purpose flour
1 tbsp. tomato paste
3¾ cups beef stock
salt and freshly ground black pepper
1 fresh bay leaf
2½ cups sliced carrots
12 oz. baby new potatoes, scrubbed
6½ cups chopped fresh
   spinach leaves

For the dumplings:

1 cup self-rising flour
¼ cup shredded suet or
   vegetable shortening
1 tbsp. freshly chopped mixed herbs
2–3 tbsp. water

Italian Pot Roast

1   Preheat the oven to 300°F. Put the beef, onions, garlic, celery, and carrots in a bowl. Place the tomatoes in a separate bowl and cover with boiling water. Let stand for 2 minutes, then drain. Peel away the skins, discard the seeds, and chop, then add, along with the red wine, to the bowl with the beef mixture. Cover tightly and marinate in the refrigerator overnight.

2   Lift the marinated beef from the bowl and pat dry with absorbent paper towels. Heat the olive oil in a large casserole dish, cook the beef until it is browned all over, and then remove from the dish. Drain the vegetables from the marinade and set the marinade aside. Add the vegetables to the casserole dish and cook gently for 5 minutes, stirring occasionally, until all the vegetables are browned.

3   Return the beef to the casserole dish with the marinade, beef stock, tomato paste, and mixed herbs, and season to taste with salt and pepper. Bring to a boil, then cover and cook in the preheated oven for 3 hours.

4   Using a slotted spoon, transfer the beef and any large vegetables to a plate, and leave in a warm place. Blend the butter and flour to form a paste. Bring the casserole juices to a boil and then gradually stir in small spoonfuls of the paste. Cook until thickened. Serve immediately with the sauce and a selection of vegetables.

Ingredients   SERVES 6

4 lb. brisket of beef
1 cup peeled small onions
3 garlic cloves, peeled and chopped
2 celery stalks, trimmed and chopped
2 carrots, peeled and sliced
3 medium, ripe tomatoes
$1^{1}/_{4}$ cups Italian red wine
2 tbsp. olive oil
$1^{1}/_{4}$ cups beef stock
1 tbsp. tomato paste
2 tsp. dried mixed herbs
salt and freshly ground black pepper
2 tbsp. butter
$^{1}/_{4}$ cup all-purpose flour
freshly cooked vegetables, to serve

Helpful hint

Many supermarkets do not sell brisket, but good butchers will be able to order it. Brisket is an excellent cut for all kinds of pot roasts, but make sure it is professionally trimmed, as it can contain a lot of gristle and fat.

Chili Con Carne with Crispy-Skinned Potatoes

1 Preheat the oven to 350°F. Heat the oil in a large, flameproof casserole dish and add the onion. Cook gently for 10 minutes until soft and lightly browned. Add the garlic and chile, and cook briefly. Increase the heat. Add the steak or ground beef and cook for an additional 10 minutes, stirring occasionally, until browned.

2 Add the chili powder and stir well. Cook for about 2 minutes, then add the chopped tomatoes and tomato paste. Bring slowly to a boil. Cover and cook in the preheated oven for 1½ hours. Remove from the oven and stir in the kidney beans. Return to the oven for an additional 15 minutes.

3 Meanwhile, brush a little vegetable oil all over the potatoes and rub on some coarse salt. Put the potatoes in the oven alongside the chili.

4 Remove the chili from the oven and stir in the kidney beans. Return to the oven for an additional 15 minutes.

5 Cut a cross in each potato, then squeeze to open slightly, and season to taste with salt and pepper. Serve with the chili, guacamole, and sour cream.

Ingredients   SERVES 4

2 tbsp. vegetable oil, plus extra
   for brushing
1 large onion, peeled and
   finely chopped
1 garlic clove, peeled and
   finely chopped
1 red chile, seeded and
   finely chopped
1 lb. chuck steak, finely chopped,
   or lean ground beef
1 tbsp. chili powder
14 oz. canned chopped tomatoes
2 tbsp. tomato paste
14 oz. canned red kidney beans,
   drained and rinsed
4 large baking potatoes
coarse salt and freshly ground
   black pepper

To serve:
guacamole
sour cream

Beef Fajitas with Avocado Salsa

1 Heat the wok, add the oil, then stir-fry the beef for 3–4 minutes. Add the garlic and spices, and cook for an additional 2 minutes. Stir the tomatoes into the wok, bring to a boil, cover, and simmer gently for 5 minutes.

2 Meanwhile, blend the kidney beans in a food processor until slightly broken up, then add to the wok. Continue to cook for an additional 5 minutes, adding 2–3 tablespoons water. The mixture should be thick and fairly dry. Stir in the chopped cilantro.

3 Mix the chopped avocado, shallot, tomato, chile, and lemon juice together. Spoon into a serving dish and set aside.

4 When ready to serve, warm the flour tortillas and spread with a little sour cream. Place a spoonful of the beef mixture on top, followed by a spoonful of the avocado sauce, then roll up. Repeat until all the mixture is used up. Serve immediately with a green salad.

Ingredients   SERVES 3–6

2 tbsp. corn oil
1 lb. rump steak, trimmed and
    cut into strips
2 garlic cloves, peeled and crushed
1 tsp. ground cumin
$^{1}/_{4}$ tsp. cayenne pepper
1 tbsp. paprika
8 oz. canned chopped tomatoes
7 oz. canned red kidney
    beans, drained
1 tbsp. freshly chopped cilantro
1 avocado, peeled, pitted,
    and chopped
1 shallot, peeled and chopped
1 large tomato, peeled, seeded,
    and chopped
1 red chile, diced
1 tbsp. lemon juice
6 large flour tortillas
3–4 tbsp. sour cream
green salad, to serve

Lamb & Date Tagine

1 Place the saffron in a small bowl, cover with warm water, and let steep for 10 minutes. Heat the oil in a large, heavy pan, add the onion, garlic, and lamb, and sauté for 8–10 minutes until sealed. Add the cinnamon stick and ground cumin and cook, stirring continuously, for an additional 2 minutes.

2 Add the carrots and sweet potatoes, then add the saffron with the soaking liquid and the stock. Bring to a boil, season to taste with salt and pepper, then reduce the heat to a simmer. Cover with a lid and simmer for 45 minutes, stirring occasionally.

3 Add the dates and continue to simmer for an additional 15 minutes. Remove the cinnamon stick, adjust the seasoning, and serve with freshly prepared couscous.

Ingredients   SERVES 4

few saffron strands
1 tbsp. olive oil
1 onion, peeled and cut into wedges
2–3 garlic cloves, peeled and sliced
1¼ lb. lean lamb, such as fillet of neck, diced
1 cinnamon stick, bruised
1 tsp. ground cumin
1¾ cups sliced carrots
2⅔ cups diced sweet potatoes
3¾ cups lamb or vegetable stock
salt and freshly ground black pepper
1 cup pitted and halved dates (fresh or dried)
freshly prepared couscous, to serve

Tasty tip
Replace the dates with chopped ready-to-eat dried apricots.

Lamb & Potato Casserole

1 Preheat the oven to 325°F. Trim any excess fat from the lamb. Heat the oil in a skillet, and brown the pieces of lamb in batches for 3–4 minutes each. Remove with a slotted spoon and set aside. Add the onions to the pan and cook for 6–8 minutes until softened and just beginning to brown, then set aside.

2 Stir in the flour and cook for a few seconds, then gradually pour in the stock, stirring well, and bring to a boil. Remove from the heat.

3 Spread the bottom of a large casserole dish with half the potato slices. Top with half the onions and season well with salt and pepper. Arrange the browned meat in a layer. Season again and add the remaining onions, the bay leaf, and thyme. Pour in the remaining liquid from the onions and top with the remaining potatoes so that they overlap in a single layer. Brush the potatoes with the melted butter and season again.

4 Cover and cook in the preheated oven for 2 hours. Uncover for the last 30 minutes to brown the potatoes. Garnish with chopped herbs and serve immediately with green beans.

Ingredients SERVES 4

$2^1/_4$ lb. neck slices or rib chops of lamb
2 tbsp. vegetable oil
2 large onions, peeled and sliced
2 tsp. all-purpose flour
$^2/_3$ cup vegetable or lamb stock
$3^3/_4$ cups peeled and thickly sliced waxy potatoes
salt and freshly ground black pepper
1 bay leaf
2 fresh thyme sprigs
1 tbsp. melted butter
2 tbsp. freshly chopped herbs, to garnish
freshly cooked green beans, to serve

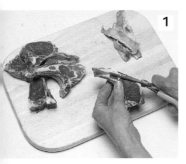

Lamb Pilaf

1 Preheat the oven to 325°F. Heat the oil in a flameproof casserole dish with a tight-fitting lid, and add the almonds. Cook, stirring often, for about 1 minute, until just browning. Add the onion, carrot, and celery, and cook gently for an additional 8–10 minutes until soft and lightly browned.

2 Increase the heat and add the lamb. Cook for an additional 5 minutes until the lamb has changed color. Add the ground cinnamon and pepper flakes. Stir briefly before adding the tomatoes and orange zest.

3 Stir and add the rice, then the stock. Bring slowly to a boil and cover tightly. Transfer to the preheated oven and cook for 30–35 minutes until rice is tender and the stock is absorbed.

4 Remove from the oven and leave for 5 minutes before stirring in the chives and cilantro. Season to taste with salt and pepper. Garnish with the lemon slices and sprigs of cilantro, and serve immediately.

Ingredients   SERVES 4

2 tbsp. vegetable oil
$^1/_4$ cup flaked or slivered almonds
1 medium onion, peeled and
   finely chopped
1 medium carrot, peeled and
   finely chopped
1 celery stalk, trimmed and
   finely chopped
$^3/_4$ lb. lean lamb, cut into chunks
$^1/_4$ tsp. ground cinnamon
$^1/_4$ tsp. pepper flakes
2 large tomatoes, skinned, deseeded,
   and chopped
grated zest of 1 orange
2 cups easy-cook brown basmati rice
$2^1/_2$ cups vegetable or lamb stock
2 tbsp. freshly cut chives
3 tbsp. freshly chopped cilantro
salt and freshly ground black pepper

To garnish:
lemon slices
sprigs of cilantro

Lamb & Vegetable Soup

1 Put the lamb in a large saucepan, cover with cold water, and bring to a boil. Add a generous pinch of salt. Simmer gently for 1¹/₂ hours, then set aside to cool completely, preferably overnight.

2 The next day, skim the fat off the surface of the lamb liquid and discard. Return the saucepan to the heat and bring back to a boil. Simmer for 5 minutes. Add the onions, potatoes, parsnips, rutabaga, and carrots, and return to a boil. Reduce the heat, cover, and cook for about 20 minutes, stirring occasionally.

3 Add the leeks and season to taste with salt and pepper. Cook for an additional 10 minutes, or until all the vegetables are tender.

4 Using a slotted spoon, remove the meat from the saucepan and, when cool, take it off the bone. Discard the bones and any gristle, then return the meat to the pan. Adjust the seasoning to taste, stir in the parsley, then serve immediately with plenty of warm, crusty bread.

Ingredients SERVES 4–6

1¹/₂ lb. neck slices or rib chops
  of lamb
pinch salt
2 large onions, peeled and
  thinly sliced
3 large potatoes, peeled and
  cut into chunks
2 parsnips, peeled and
  cut into chunks
1 rutabaga, peeled and
  cut into chunks
3 large carrots, peeled and cut
  into chunks
2 leeks, trimmed and sliced
salt freshly ground black pepper
4 tbsp. freshly chopped parsley
warm, crusty bread, to serve

Cassoulet

1 Preheat the oven to 350°F. Heat the oil in a large saucepan or flameproof casserole dish, add the onion, celery, carrots, and garlic, and sauté for 5 minutes.

2 Cut the pork, if using, into small pieces and cut the sausages into chunks. Add the meat to the vegetables and cook, stirring, until lightly browned.

3 Add the thyme sprigs and season to taste with salt and pepper. If a saucepan was used, transfer everything to a casserole dish.

4 Spoon the beans on top, then pour in the stock. Mix the bread crumbs with 1 tablespoon of the chopped thyme in a small bowl and sprinkle on top of the beans. Cover with a lid and cook in the oven for 40 minutes. Remove the lid and cook for an additional 15 minutes, or until the bread crumbs are crisp. Sprinkle with the remaining chopped thyme and serve.

Ingredients   SERVES 4

1 tbsp. olive oil
1 onion, peeled and chopped
2 celery stalks, trimmed and chopped
1½ cups sliced carrots
2–3 garlic cloves, peeled and crushed
12 oz. pork belly (optional)
8 thick, spicy link sausages,
    such as Toulouse
few fresh thyme sprigs
salt and freshly ground black pepper
28 oz. canned cannellini beans,
    drained and rinsed
2½ cups vegetable stock
1⅔ cups fresh bread crumbs
2 tbsp. freshly chopped thyme

Tasty tip

Replace the pork belly with lardons, if you prefer.

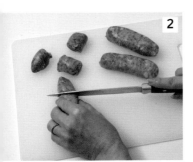

Sausage & Apple Casserole

1 Preheat the oven to 350°F. Heat the oil in a flameproof casserole dish (or skillet, if preferred), add the onion, garlic, and celery, and sauté for 5 minutes. Push the vegetables to one side, then add the sausages and cook, turning the sausages over, until browned.

2 If a skillet has been used, transfer everything to an ovenproof dish. Arrange the onions over and around the sausages, together with the carrots, apple, and zucchini. Season to taste with salt and pepper and pour over the stock. Sprinkle with the mixed herbs, cover with a lid, and cook in the oven for 30 minutes.

3 Meanwhile, soak the grated potatoes in a bowl of cold water for 10 minutes. Drain thoroughly, then place the potatoes on a clean dish towel and squeeze to remove any excess moisture.

4 Remove the casserole dish from the oven and place the grated potatoes on top. Sprinkle with the grated cheese, then return to the oven and cook for 30 minutes, or until the vegetables are tender and the topping is crisp.

Ingredients   SERVES 4

1 tbsp. olive oil
1 onion, peeled and sliced
2–3 garlic cloves, peeled and sliced
2 celery stalks, trimmed and sliced
8 apple-and-pork-flavored thick
   link sausages
$1^{1}/_{2}$ cups sliced carrots
1 large baking apple, peeled
   and sliced
$2^{3}/_{4}$ cups sliced zucchini
salt and freshly ground black pepper
$2^{1}/_{2}$ cups vegetable stock
2 tsp. dried mixed herbs
3 cups peeled and grated potatoes
$^{1}/_{2}$ cup grated Gruyère cheese

New Orleans Jambalaya

1   Mix all the seasoning ingredients together in a small bowl and set aside.

2   Heat 2 tablespoons of the oil in a large, flameproof casserole dish over medium heat. Add the ham and sausage, and cook, stirring often, for 7–8 minutes until golden. Remove from the pan and set aside.

3   Add the remaining oil and the onions, celery, and bell peppers to the casserole dish and cook for about 4 minutes until softened, stirring occasionally. Stir in the garlic, then, using a slotted spoon, transfer all the vegetables to a plate and set aside with the sausage.

4   Add the chicken pieces to the casserole dish and cook for about 4 minutes until beginning to brown, turning once. Stir in the seasoning mix and turn the pieces to coat well. Return the sausage and vegetables to the dish and stir well. Add the chopped tomatoes with their juice and the stock, and bring to a boil.

5   Stir in the rice and reduce the heat to low. Cover and simmer for 12 minutes. Stir in the scallions and shrimp, and cook, covered, for an additional 4 minutes. Add the crabmeat and gently stir in. Cook for 2–3 minutes until the rice is tender. Remove from the heat, cover, and let stand for 5 minutes before serving.

Ingredients   SERVES 6–8

For the seasoning mix:

2 dried bay leaves
1 tsp. salt
2 tsp. cayenne pepper
2 tsp. dried oregano
1 tsp. each ground white and black
    pepper, or to taste
3 tbsp. vegetable oil

For the Jambalaya:

$1^{1}/_{4}$ cups diced cooked ham
$^{1}/_{2}$ lb. smoked pork link sausages, cut
    into chunks
2 large onions, peeled and chopped
4 celery stalks, trimmed and chopped
2 green bell peppers, seeded
    and chopped
2 garlic cloves, peeled and finely chopped
12 oz. chicken, diced
14 oz. canned chopped tomatoes
$2^{1}/_{2}$ cups fish stock
$2^{1}/_{3}$ cups long-grain white rice
4 scallions, trimmed and coarsely chopped
12 oz. shrimp, peeled
8 oz. white crabmeat

Oven-Roasted Vegetables with Sausages

1 Preheat the oven to 400°F. Cut the eggplants and zucchini into bite-size chunks. Line a large roasting pan with foil and pour in the olive oil, then heat in the preheated oven for 3 minutes, or until very hot. Add the eggplants, zucchini, and garlic cloves, stir until coated in the hot oil, and cook in the oven for 10 minutes.

2 Remove the roasting pan from the oven and stir. Lightly prick the sausages, add to the roasting pan, and return to the oven. Continue to roast for an additional 20 minutes, turning once during cooking, until the vegetables are tender and the sausages are golden brown.

3 Meanwhile, coarsely chop the plum tomatoes and drain the canellini beans. Remove the sausages from the oven and stir in the tomatoes and canellini beans. Season to taste with salt and pepper, then return to the oven for 5 minutes, or until heated thoroughly.

4 Sprinkle with the torn basil leaves, plenty of grated Parmesan cheese, and extra freshly ground black pepper. Serve immediately.

Ingredients   SERVES 4

2 medium eggplants, trimmed
3 medium zucchini, trimmed
$1/4$ cup olive oil
6 garlic cloves
8 Italian-style link sausages
4 plum tomatoes
22 oz. canned canellini beans
salt and freshly ground black pepper
1 bunch fresh basil, torn into
    coarse pieces
4 tbsp. Parmesan cheese, grated

Helpful hint

By leaving the garlic cloves unpeeled, a more delicate flavor is achieved. If a more robust flavor is required, peel the garlic before cooking.

Pork Goulash

1 Preheat the oven to 325°F. Cut the pork into large cubes, about 1¹/₂ inches square. Heat the oil in a large, flameproof casserole dish and brown the pork in batches over high heat, transferring the cubes to a plate as they brown.

2 Over medium heat, add the onions and bell pepper, and cook for about 5 minutes, stirring regularly, until they begin to brown. Add the garlic and return the meat to the casserole along with any juices on the plate. Sprinkle in the flour and paprika and stir well to soak up the oil and juices.

3 Add the tomatoes and season to taste with salt and pepper. Bring slowly to a boil, cover with a tight-fitting lid, and cook in the preheated oven for 1¹/₂–2 hours until tender. Heat the rice according to the package directions.

4 When the meat is tender, stir in the sour cream to create a marbled effect, or serve separately. Garnish with parsley and serve with the rice.

Ingredients   SERVES 6

1¹/₂ lb. boneless pork rib chops
1 tbsp. olive oil
2 onions, peeled and
    coarsely chopped
1 red bell pepper, seeded and
    thinly sliced
1 garlic clove, peeled and crushed
1 tbsp. all-purpose flour
heaping 1 tbsp. paprika
14 oz. canned chopped tomatoes
salt and freshly ground black pepper
18 oz. packaged microwaveable
    long-grain white rice
²/₃ cup sour cream, to serve
fresh Italian parsley sprigs,
    to garnish

Food fact

Paprika is the ground red powder from the dried pepper *Capsicum annum* and is a vital ingredient of goulash, giving it a distinctive color and taste.

Spanish-Style Pork Stew

1 Preheat the oven to 325°F. Heat the oil in a large, flameproof casserole dish and add the pork in batches. Fry over high heat until browned. Transfer each batch to a plate until all the pork is browned.

2 Reduce the heat and add the onion to the casserole dish. Cook for 5 minutes until soft and starting to brown. Add the garlic. Stir briefly before returning the pork to the casserole dish. Add the flour and stir.

3 Add the tomatoes. Gradually stir in the red wine and add the basil. Bring to simmering point and cover. Transfer the casserole dish to the lower part of the preheated oven and cook for 1$^1/_2$ hours. Stir in the green bell pepper and olives, and cook for an additional 30 minutes or until tender. Season to taste with salt and pepper. Heat the rice according to the package instructions and serve with the stew, garnished with fresh basil.

Ingredients
SERVES 4

2 tbsp. olive oil
2 lb. lean, boneless pork, diced
1 large onion, peeled and sliced
2 garlic cloves, peeled and
   finely chopped
1 tbsp. all-purpose flour
1 lb. plum tomatoes, peeled
   and chopped
$^3/_4$ cup red wine
1 tbsp. freshly chopped basil
1 green bell pepper, seeded
   and sliced
$^1/_2$ cup crosswise-halved pimento-
   stuffed olives
salt and freshly ground black pepper
fresh basil leaves, to garnish
2 9-oz. packages microwaveable
   basmati rice

Pork Chop Casserole

1 Preheat the oven to 375 F. Trim the pork chops, removing any excess fat, wipe with a clean, damp cloth, then dust with a little flour and set aside. Cut the shallots in half, if large. Chop the garlic and slice the sun-dried tomatoes.

2 Heat the olive oil in a large casserole dish and cook the pork chops for 5–8 minutes until sealed, turning once. Using a slotted spoon, carefully lift out of the dish and set aside. Add the shallots and cook for 5 minutes, stirring occasionally.

3 Return the pork chops to the casserole dish and sprinkle with the garlic and sun-dried tomatoes, then pour over the canned tomatoes with their juice.

4 Blend the red wine, stock, and tomato paste together, and add the chopped oregano. Season to taste with salt and pepper, then pour over the pork chops and bring to a gentle boil. Cover with a close-fitting lid and cook in the preheated oven for 20 minutes. Add the potatoes (if using at this point) to the casserole dish and continue to cook for 40 minutes, or until the pork chops and potatoes are tender. Adjust the seasoning to taste, sprinkle with a few oregano leaves, and serve immediately with separate new potatoes (if preferred) and green beans, if liked.

Ingredients   SERVES 4

4 pork chops
flour, for dusting
1 cup peeled shallots
2 garlic cloves, peeled
$1/_4$ cup sun-dried tomatoes
2 tbsp. olive oil
14 oz. canned plum tomatoes
$2/_3$ cup red wine
$2/_3$ cup chicken stock
3 tbsp. tomato paste
2 tbsp. freshly chopped oregano
salt and freshly ground black pepper
1 lb. new potatoes, scrubbed and
    halved, if large (optional, see below)
fresh oregano leaves, to garnish
freshly cooked new potatoes, to
    serve (if preferred separately)
green beans, to serve (optional)

Oven-Baked Pork Balls with Peppers

1 Preheat the oven to 400°F. If making your own garlic bread, crush the garlic, then blend with the softened butter, the parsley, and enough lemon juice to give a soft consistency. Shape into a roll, wrap in parchment paper, and chill in the refrigerator for at least 30 minutes.

2 Mix together the pork, basil, 1 chopped garlic clove, sun-dried tomatoes, and seasoning until well combined. With damp hands, roll into 16 balls and set aside.

3 Spoon the olive oil into a large roasting pan (lined with foil if liked) and place in the preheated oven for about 3 minutes until very hot. Remove from the oven and stir in the pork balls, the remaining chopped garlic, and bell peppers. Cook for about 15 minutes. Remove from the oven, stir in the cherry tomatoes, and season to taste with plenty of salt and pepper. Cook for an additional 20 minutes.

4 Just before the pork balls are ready, either heat the bought garlic bread (if using) according to package directions, or, if making your own, slice the bread, toast lightly, and spread with the prepared garlic butter. Remove the pork balls from the oven, stir in the vinegar, and serve immediately with the garlic bread.

Ingredients   SERVES 4

For the garlic bread (optional):
2–4 garlic cloves, peeled
4 tbsp. butter, softened
1 tbsp. freshly chopped parsley
2–3 tsp. lemon juice
1 focaccia loaf

For the pork balls:
2 cups fresh ground pork
4 tbsp. freshly chopped basil
2 garlic cloves, peeled and chopped
3 sun-dried tomatoes, chopped
salt and freshly ground black pepper
3 tbsp. olive oil
1 medium red bell pepper, seeded
   and cut into chunks
1 medium green bell pepper, seeded
   and cut into chunks
1 medium yellow bell pepper, seeded
   and cut into chunks
2 cups cherry tomatoes
2 tbsp. balsamic vinegar

bought garlic bread, to serve (if not
   making own)

Italian Risotto

1 Chop the onion and garlic and set aside. Heat the olive oil in a large skillet, and cook the salami for 3–5 minutes until golden. Transfer to a plate and keep warm. Add the asparagus and stir-fry for 2–3 minutes until just wilted. Transfer to the plate with the salami. Add the onion and garlic, and cook for 5 minutes, or until softened.

2 Add the rice to the skillet and cook for 2 minutes. Add the wine, bring to a boil, then simmer, stirring, until the wine has been absorbed. Add half the stock and return to a boil. Simmer, stirring, until the liquid has been absorbed.

3 Add half the remaining stock and the fava beans to the rice mixture. Bring to a boil, then simmer for an additional 5–10 minutes until all the liquid has been absorbed.

4 Add the remaining stock, bring to a boil, then simmer until all the liquid is absorbed and the rice is tender. Stir in the remaining ingredients until the cheese has just melted. Serve immediately.

Ingredients   SERVES 4

1 onion, peeled
2 garlic cloves, peeled
1 tbsp. olive oil
2 cups Italian salami, chopped
$^1/_2$ cup asparagus tips
$1^1/_2$ cups risotto rice
$1^1/_4$ cups dry white wine
4 cups chicken stock, warmed
$^3/_4$ cup thawed frozen fava beans
1 cup diced dolcelatte or blue cheese
3 tbsp. freshly chopped mixed herbs, such as parsley and basil
salt and freshly ground black pepper

Food fact

Cheese is a common constituent in the making of risotto and helps to provide some of its creamy texture. Usually Parmesan cheese is added at the end of cooking, but here a good-quality Dolcelatte is used instead.

Risi e Bisi

1 Melt the butter and olive oil together in a large, heavy saucepan. Add the chopped pancetta or bacon, the chopped onion and garlic, and cook gently for about 10 minutes until the onion is softened and is just beginning to brown.

2 Pour in the vegetable stock, then add the sugar, lemon juice, and bay leaf. Bring the mixture to a fast boil.

3 Add the rice, stir, and simmer uncovered for about 20 minutes until the rice is tender. Occasionally, stir the mixture gently while it cooks. Stir the peas into the rice about 2 minutes before the end of the cooking time.

4 When the rice is cooked, remove the bay leaf and discard. Stir in $2^1/_2$ tablespoons of the chopped parsley and the Parmesan cheese. Season to taste with salt and pepper.

5 Transfer the rice to a large serving dish. Garnish with the remaining chopped parsley, a sprig of fresh parsley, and julienned strips of orange zest. Serve immediately while piping hot.

Ingredients   SERVES 4

2 tbsp. unsalted butter
1 tsp. olive oil
3 slices pancetta or bacon, chopped
1 small onion, peeled and
    finely chopped
1 garlic clove, peeled and
    finely chopped
$5^1/_4$ cups vegetable stock
pinch superfine sugar
1 tsp. lemon juice
1 bay leaf
1 cup risotto rice
$1^1/_2$ cups thawed frozen peas
3 tbsp. freshly chopped parsley
$^1/_2$ cup finely grated Parmesan cheese
salt and freshly ground black pepper

To garnish:

fresh parsley sprig
julienned strips of orange zest

Leek & Ham Risotto

1 Heat the oil and half the butter together in a large saucepan. Add the onion and leeks, and cook over a medium heat for 6–8 minutes, stirring occasionally, until soft and beginning to color. Stir in the thyme and cook briefly.

2 Add the rice and stir well. Continue stirring over medium heat for about 1 minute until the rice is glossy. Add a ladleful or two of the stock and stir well until the stock is absorbed. Continue adding stock, a ladleful at a time, stirring well between additions, until about two-thirds of the stock has been added.

3 Meanwhile, either chop or finely shred the ham, then add to the saucepan of rice, together with the peas. Continue adding ladlefuls of stock, as described in step 2, until the rice is tender and the ham is heated through completely.

4 Add the remaining butter, sprinkle with the Parmesan cheese, and season to taste with salt and pepper. When the butter has melted and the cheese has softened, stir well to incorporate. Taste and adjust the seasoning, then serve immediately.

Ingredients   SERVES 4

1 tbsp. olive oil
2 tbsp. butter
1 medium onion, peeled and
   finely chopped
4 leeks, trimmed and thinly sliced
1$\frac{1}{2}$ tbsp. freshly chopped thyme
2 cups Arborio rice
5$\frac{1}{2}$ cups heated vegetable or
   chicken stock
$\frac{1}{2}$ lb. cooked ham
1$\frac{1}{4}$ cups peas, thawed if frozen
$\frac{1}{2}$ cup grated Parmesan cheese
salt and freshly ground black pepper

Helpful hint

Risotto should take about 20–25 minutes to cook, so taste it after this time—the rice should be creamy, with just a slight bite to it. If it is not quite ready, continue adding the stock, a little at a time, and cook for a few more minutes. Stop as soon as it tastes ready, as you do not have to add all of the liquid.

Sausage & Bacon Risotto

1 Heat a wok or large skillet, pour in the oil, and melt the butter. Fry the cocktail sausages, turning continuously, for 8–10 minutes until cooked. Remove with a slotted spoon, cut in half, and keep warm.

2 Add the chopped shallot and bacon to the wok or skillet and fry for 2–3 minutes until cooked but not browned. Add the chorizo or spicy sausage and green bell pepper and stir-fry for an additional 3 minutes.

3 Add the cold rice and the corn to the wok or skillet and stir-fry for 2 minutes, then return the cooked sausages and cook over the heat until everything is piping hot. Garnish with the freshly chopped parsley and serve immediately.

Ingredients   SERVES 4

1 tbsp. olive oil
2 tbsp. butter
4 cocktail or small link sausages
1 shallot, peeled and finely chopped
3 oz. thick slices bacon, chopped
5 oz. chorizo or similar spicy sausage, cut into chunks
1 green bell pepper, seeded and cut into strips
scant 2 cups cold pre-cooked long-grain rice
7 oz. canned corn kernels, drained
2 tbsp. freshly chopped parsley

Helpful hint

It is now possible to buy packages of bacon or pancetta lardons, but if these are unavailable, try to get bacon in a piece from a butcher or deli. Cut the bacon into $1/2$ inch slices, then cut the slices widthwise into $1/2$ inch pieces.

Honey Pork with Rice Noodles & Cashews

1 Soak the rice noodles in boiling water for 4 minutes, or according to the package directions. Drain and set aside.

2 Trim and slice the pork fillet into thin strips. Heat the wok, add the oil and butter, and stir-fry the pork for 4–5 minutes until cooked. Remove with a slotted spoon and keep warm.

3 Add the onion to the wok and stir-fry for 2 minutes. Stir in the garlic and mushrooms and cook for an additional 2 minutes, or until juices start to run from the mushrooms.

4 Blend the soy sauce with the honey, then return the pork to the wok with this mixture. Add the cashews and cook for 1–2 minutes, then add the rice noodles, a little at a time. Stir-fry until everything is piping hot. Sprinkle with chopped chile and scallions. Serve immediately with freshly stir-fried vegetables.

Ingredients   SERVES 4

$1^2/_3$ cups rice noodles
1 lb. pork fillet
2 tbsp. peanut oil
1 tbsp. butter, softened
1 onion, peeled and finely sliced
   into rings
2 garlic cloves, peeled and crushed
1 cup baby button mushrooms, halved
3 tbsp. light soy sauce
3 tbsp. honey
$^1/_2$ cup unsalted cashews
1 red chile, seeded and finely chopped
4 scallions, trimmed and
   finely chopped
freshly stir-fried vegetables, to serve

Pork with Tofu & Coconut

1 Place the cashews, coriander, cumin, chili powder, ginger, and oyster sauce in a food processor and blend until well ground. Heat a wok or large skillet, add 2 tablespoons of the oil, and, when hot, add the cashew mixture and stir-fry for 1 minute. Stir in the coconut milk, bring to a boil, then simmer for 1 minute. Pour into a small pitcher and set aside. Wipe the wok clean.

2 Meanwhile, place the rice noodles in a bowl, cover with boiling water, let stand for 5 minutes, then drain thoroughly.

3 Reheat the wok, add the remaining oil, and, when hot, add the pork and stir-fry for 5 minutes, or until browned all over. Add the chiles and scallions and stir-fry for 2 minutes.

4 Add the tomatoes and tofu to the wok with the noodles and coconut mixture and stir-fry for an additional 2 minutes, or until heated through, being careful not to break up the tofu. Sprinkle with the chopped cilantro and mint, season to taste with salt and pepper, and stir. Tip into a warmed serving dish and serve immediately.

Ingredients   SERVES 4

1$^1/_3$ cups unsalted cashews
1 tbsp. ground coriander
1 tbsp. ground cumin
2 tsp. hot chili powder
1-in. piece ginger, peeled
    and chopped
1 tbsp. oyster sauce
4 tbsp. peanut oil
1$^3/_4$ cups coconut milk
6 oz. rice noodles
1 lb. pork tenderloin, thickly sliced
1 red chile, deseeded and sliced
1 green chile, deseeded and sliced
1 bunch scallions, trimmed and
    thickly sliced
3 tomatoes, coarsely chopped
3 oz. tofu, drained
2 tbsp. freshly chopped cilantro
2 tbsp. freshly chopped mint
salt and freshly ground black pepper

Poultry & Game

Tired of just meat and potatoes? Bored of beef? Try something new with such delectable poultry dishes as Chicken & White Wine Risotto or Persian Chicken Pilaf. Guaranteed, mouths will water for Creamy Caribbean Chicken & Coconut Soup, but, if chicken's not your game, then Turkey Cutlets Marsala with Wilted Watercress is a must try.

Wonton Noodle Soup

1 Place the mushrooms in a bowl, cover with warm water, and let soak for 1 hour. Drain, remove, and discard the stalks, and finely chop the mushrooms. Return to the bowl with the shrimp, pork, water chestnuts, 2 of the scallions, and the egg white. Season to taste with salt and pepper. Mix well.

2 Mix the cornstarch with 1 tablespoon cold water to make a paste. Place a wonton wrapper on a board and brush the edges with the paste. Drop a little less than 1 teaspoon of the pork mixture in the center, then fold in half to make a triangle, pressing the edges together. Bring the two outer corners together, pressing together with a little more paste. Continue until all the pork mixture is used up; you should have 16–20 wontons.

3 Pour the stock into a large, wide saucepan, add the ginger slices, and bring to a boil. Add the wontons and simmer for about 5 minutes. Add the noodles and cook for 1 minute. Stir in the bok choy and cook for an additional 2 minutes, or until the noodles and bok choy are tender, and the wontons have floated to the surface and are cooked through.

4 Ladle the soup into warmed bowls, discarding the ginger. Sprinkle with the remaining sliced scallions and serve immediately.

Ingredients   SERVES 4

4 dried shiitake mushrooms, wiped
$3/4$ cup peeled and finely chopped raw shrimp
$1/4$ lb. ground pork
4 water chestnuts, finely chopped
4 scallions, trimmed and finely sliced
1 large egg white
salt and freshly ground black pepper
$1^1/_2$ tsp. cornstarch
1 package fresh wonton wrappers
5 cups chicken stock
$3/4$-in. piece ginger, peeled and sliced
3 oz. thin egg noodles
1 cup shredded bok choy

Food fact

Wonton wrappers are thin sheets, about 4 in. square, of noodle dough made from eggs and flour. Buy them fresh or frozen from larger supermarkets and Asian markets.

Clear Chicken & Mushroom Soup

1 Skin the chicken legs and remove any fat. Cut each in half to make 2 thigh and 2 drumstick portions, and set aside. Heat the peanut and sesame oils in a large saucepan. Add the sliced onion and cook gently for 10 minutes, or until soft but not beginning to brown.

2 Add the chopped ginger to the saucepan, and cook for about 30 seconds, stirring continuously to prevent it from sticking, then pour in the stock. Add the chicken and the lemongrass, cover, and simmer gently for 15 minutes. Stir in the rice and cook for an additional 15 minutes, or until the chicken is cooked.

3 Remove the chicken from the saucepan and leave until cool enough to handle. Finely shred the flesh, then return to the saucepan with the mushrooms, scallions, soy sauce, and sherry. Simmer for 5 minutes, or until the rice and mushrooms are tender. Remove the lemongrass.

4 Season the soup to taste with pepper. Ladle into warmed serving bowls, making sure each has an equal amount of shredded chicken and vegetables, and serve immediately.

Ingredients   SERVES 4

2 large chicken legs, about
    1 lb. total weight
1 tbsp. peanut oil
1 tsp. sesame oil
1 onion, peeled and very thinly sliced
1 in. piece ginger, peeled and very
    finely chopped
5 cups clear chicken stock
1 lemongrass stalk, bruised
$\frac{1}{3}$ cup long-grain rice
1 cup wiped and finely sliced
    button mushrooms
4 scallions, trimmed, cut into
    2-in. pieces, and shredded
1 tbsp. dark soy sauce
4 tbsp. dry sherry
freshly ground black pepper

Chinese Chicken Soup

1 Remove any skin from the chicken. Place on a cutting board and use two forks to tear the chicken into fine shreds.

2 Heat the oil in a large saucepan and fry the scallions and chile for 1 minute. Add the garlic and ginger and cook for another minute. Stir in the chicken stock and gradually bring the mixture to a boil.

3 Break up the noodles a little and add to the boiling stock along with the carrot. Stir to mix, then reduce the heat to a simmer and cook for 3–4 minutes.

4 Add the shredded chicken, bean sprouts, soy sauce, and fish sauce, and stir.

5 Cook for an additional 2–3 minutes until piping hot. Spoon the soup into bowls and sprinkle with a few fresh cilantro leaves. Serve immediately.

Ingredients   SERVES 4

2 cooked chicken breasts or thighs
1 tsp. vegetable oil
6 scallions, trimmed and
    diagonally sliced
1 red chile, seeded and
    finely chopped
1 garlic clove, peeled and crushed
1-in. piece fresh ginger, peeled and
    finely grated
4 cups chicken stock
$1^1/_2$ cups medium egg noodles
1 carrot, peeled and cut
    into matchsticks
$^3/_4$ cup bean sprouts
2 tbsp. soy sauce
1 tbsp. Thai fish sauce
fresh cilantro leaves, to garnish

Tasty tip

If possible, buy corn-fed chicken for this recipe. Since this soup is chicken stock-based, the use of corn-fed chicken will make the soup much more flavorsome.

Creamy Caribbean Chicken & Coconut Soup

1 Trim the scallions and slice thinly; peel the garlic and chop finely. Cut off the top from the chile, slit down the side and remove the seeds and membrane, then chop finely and set aside. Remove and discard any skin or bones from the cooked chicken and shred, using two forks, and set aside.

2 Heat a large wok, add the oil, and, when hot, add the scallions, garlic, and chili, and stir-fry for 2 minutes, or until the scallions have softened. Stir in the turmeric and cook for 1 minute.

3 Blend the coconut milk with the chicken stock until smooth, then pour into the wok. Add the pasta or spaghetti with the lemon slices, and bring to a boil.

4 Simmer, half covered, for 10–12 minutes until the pasta is tender; stir occasionally.

5 Remove the lemon slices from the wok and add the chicken. Season to taste with salt and pepper, and simmer for 2–3 minutes until the chicken is heated through. Stir in the chopped cilantro and ladle into heated bowls. Garnish with sprigs of fresh cilantro and serve immediately.

Ingredients SERVES 4

6–8 scallions
2 garlic cloves
1 red chile
6 oz. cooked chicken
2 tbsp. vegetable oil
1 tsp. ground turmeric
1 cup coconut milk
3 cups chicken stock
$^1/_2$ cup small soup pasta or spaghetti, broken into small pieces
$^1/_2$ lemon, sliced
salt and freshly ground black pepper
1–2 tbsp. freshly chopped cilantro
fresh cilantro sprigs, to garnish

Helpful hint

Be careful handling chiles. Either wear rubber gloves or scrub your hands with plenty of soap and water. Avoid touching your eyes and any other sensitive areas.

Coconut Chicken Soup

1 Discard the outer leaves of the lemongrass stalks, then place on a cutting board and, using a mallet or rolling pin, pound gently to bruise; set aside.

2 Heat the vegetable oil in a large saucepan and cook the onions over medium heat for about 10–15 minutes until soft and beginning to change color.

3 Lower the heat, stir in the garlic, ginger, lime leaves, and turmeric, and cook for 1 minute. Add the red bell pepper, coconut milk, stock, lemongrass, and rice. Bring to a boil, cover, and simmer gently over low heat for about 10 minutes.

4 Add the chicken and then stir it into the soup with the corn and the freshly chopped cilantro. Add a few dashes Thai fish sauce to taste, then reheat gently, stirring frequently. Serve immediately with a few chopped pickled chiles to sprinkle on top.

Ingredients   SERVES 4

2 lemongrass stalks
3 tbsp. vegetable oil
3 medium onions, peeled and
    finely sliced
3 garlic cloves, peeled and crushed
2 tbsp. fresh ginger, finely grated
2–3 kaffir lime leaves
1$\frac{1}{2}$ tsp. turmeric
1 red bell pepper, seeded and diced
1$\frac{3}{4}$ cups coconut milk
5 cups vegetable or chicken stock
1$\frac{1}{2}$ cups easy-cook long-grain rice
1$\frac{1}{2}$ cups coarsely diced cooked
    chicken meat
1$\frac{1}{2}$ cups corn kernels
3 tbsp. freshly chopped cilantro
1 tbsp. Thai fish sauce
freshly chopped pickled chiles,
    to serve

Food fact

If you have difficulty finding kaffir lime leaves, substitute a large strip of lime or lemon zest instead, remembering to remove before serving.

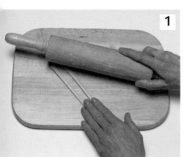

Hot & Sour Mushroom Soup

1 Place the dried shiitake mushrooms in a small bowl, and add enough almost-boiling water to cover. Leave for 20 minutes to soften, then gently lift out and squeeze out the liquid. (Lifting out the mushrooms leaves any sand and grit behind.) Discard the stems and thinly slice the caps, and set aside.

2 Heat a large wok, add the oil, and when hot, add the carrot strips and stir-fry for 2–3 minutes or until beginning to soften. Add the cremini mushrooms and stir-fry for 2–3 minutes until golden, then stir in the garlic and pepper flakes.

3 Add the chicken stock to the vegetables and bring to a boil, skimming any foam that rises to the surface. Add the shredded chicken or pork, tofu (if using), scallions, sugar, vinegar, soy sauce, and the shiitake mushrooms. Simmer for 5 minutes, stirring occasionally. Season to taste with salt and pepper.

4 Blend the cornstarch with 1 tablespoon cold water to form a smooth paste, and beat into the soup. Return to a boil and simmer over medium heat until thickened.

5 Beat the egg with the sesame oil and slowly add to the soup in a slow, steady stream, stirring continuously. Stir in the chopped cilantro and serve the soup immediately.

Ingredients SERVES 4–6

$1/4$ cup dried shiitake mushrooms

2 tbsp. peanut oil

1 carrot, peeled and cut into julienne strips

1 cup wiped and thinly sliced cremini mushrooms

2 garlic cloves, peeled and finely chopped

$1/2$ tsp. dried pepper flakes

5 cups chicken stock

1 cup shredded cooked boneless chicken or pork

$1/2$ cup thinly sliced fresh tofu (optional)

2–3 scallions, trimmed and finely sliced diagonally

1–2 tsp. sugar

3 tbsp. cider vinegar

2 tbsp. soy sauce

salt and freshly ground black pepper

1 tbsp. cornstarch

1 extra-large egg

2 tsp. sesame oil

2 tbsp. freshly chopped cilantro

Chicken Marengo Casserole

1 Preheat the oven to 350°F. Lightly rinse the chicken and pat dry with paper towels.

2 Heat the oil and butter in a flameproof casserole dish (or skillet, if preferred), add the chicken pieces, and cook until browned all over. Remove the chicken with a slotted spoon and set aside.

3 Add the onion and garlic and cook gently for 5 minutes, stirring occasionally. Sprinkle in the flour and cook for 2 minutes before stirring in the stock and bringing to a boil. If a skillet has been used, transfer the onion-and-stock mixture to an ovenproof dish.

4 Return the chicken to the dish and add the peeled tomatoes. Season to taste with salt and pepper and add the bay leaf. Cover with a lid and cook in the oven for 30 minutes. Remove the dish from the oven and add the potatoes and corn kernels. Return to the oven and cook for 30 minutes. Add the spinach and stir gently through the casserole. Return to the oven and cook for an additional 10 minutes, or until the spinach has wilted. Serve.

Ingredients   SERVES 4

4 chicken pieces, skinned
1 tbsp. olive oil
1 tbsp. unsalted butter
1 onion, peeled and cut into wedges
2–3 garlic cloves, peeled and sliced
2 tbsp. all-purpose flour
$3^3/_4$ cups chicken stock
2 medium tomatoes, peeled
salt and freshly ground black pepper
1 fresh bay leaf
12 oz. new potatoes, scrubbed and cut in half
$1/_2$ cup frozen corn kernels
12 oz. fresh spinach

Helpful hint

This can also be made using half chicken stock and half wine. Use a dry white such as Chardonnay or Pinot Grigio.

Chicken Chasseur

1 Preheat the oven to 350°F. Skin the chicken, if preferred, and rinse lightly. Pat dry with paper towels. Heat the oil and butter in a flameproof casserole dish (or skillet, if preferred), add the chicken pieces, and cook in batches until browned all over. Remove the chicken with a slotted spoon and set aside.

2 Add the onions, garlic, and celery to the casserole dish and cook for 5 minutes, or until golden. Cut the mushrooms into halves or quarters, add to the pan, and cook for 2 minutes.

3 Sprinkle in the flour and cook for 2 minutes, then gradually stir in the wine. Blend the tomato paste with a little of the stock in a small bowl, then stir into the casserole together with the remaining stock. Bring to a boil, stirring continuously.

4 If a skillet has been used, transfer the onion-and-stock mixture to an ovenproof dish.

5 Return the chicken to the casserole, season to taste, and add a few tarragon sprigs. Stir in the sweet potatoes, cover with a lid, and cook in the oven for 30 minutes. Remove the dish from the oven and add the beans. Return to the oven and cook for another 15–20 minutes until the chicken and vegetables are cooked. Serve sprinkled with chopped tarragon.

Ingredients   SERVES 4

3 lb. whole chicken, jointed into
    4 or 8 pieces
1 tbsp. olive oil
1 tbsp. unsalted butter
12 pearl onions, peeled
2–4 garlic cloves, peeled and sliced
2 celery stalks, sliced
8 medium closed-cup
    mushrooms, wiped
2 tbsp. all-purpose flour
$1^{1}/_{4}$ cups dry white wine
2 tbsp. tomato paste
2 cups chicken stock
salt and freshly ground black pepper
few fresh tarragon sprigs
$2^{2}/_{3}$ cups sweet potato chunks
2 cups shelled fresh or frozen
    fava beans
1 tbsp. freshly chopped tarragon,
    to garnish

Chicken Creole

1 Lightly rinse the chicken and pat dry with paper towels. Cut the chicken into thin strips. Heat 1 tablespoon of the oil in a deep skillet, add the chicken, and sauté for 5–7 minutes until sealed. Remove with a slotted spoon and reserve.

2 Add the remaining oil if necessary, then add the leeks, onion, garlic, and rice, and cook, stirring continuously, for 5 minutes. Add the spices and herbs and cook for an additional 5 minutes.

3 Return the chicken to the skillet and add the chopped tomatoes. Add half the stock and bring to a boil. Reduce the heat to a simmer and cook for 25 minutes, adding more stock if necessary. Stir in the okra and cook for an additional 10 minutes, then serve.

Ingredients SERVES 4

1 lb. skinless chicken breasts
1–2 tbsp. olive oil
$2^1/_2$ cups trimmed and sliced leeks
1 onion, peeled and chopped
3–4 garlic cloves, peeled and chopped
1 cup long-grain rice
$^1/_2$ tsp. cayenne pepper
$1^1/_2$ tsp. paprika
$1^1/_2$ tsp. dried oregano
$1^1/_2$ tsp. dried thyme
$1^1/_4$ cups chopped ripe tomatoes
$3^3/_4$ cups chicken stock
6 oz. okra, trimmed and sliced

Helpful hint

Okra is used frequently in Creole dishes and will help to thicken the dish slightly. If you cannot find okra, replace with sliced green beans, which, although will not thicken, will give an attractive finish to the dish.

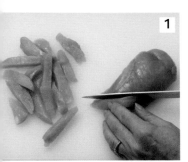

1

2

3

Chicken Gumbo

1 Rinse the chicken pieces and pat dry with paper towels. Heat the oil and butter in a large, heavy saucepan, add the chicken, and fry in batches for 8–10 minutes until lightly browned. Remove with a slotted spoon or metal tongs and set aside.

2 Add all the vegetables to the pan and sauté for 8 minutes, or until the vegetables begin to soften. Remove with a slotted spoon and set aside.

3 Add the sausages to the pan and cook for 5–8 minutes until browned all over, then remove and cut each sausage in half. Return to the pan together with the browned chicken. Add half the browned vegetables and sprinkle in the flour. Cook for 2 minutes, then gradually stir in half the stock. Bring to a boil, then reduce the heat, cover, and simmer for 40 minutes. Add the remaining vegetables together with the remaining stock and a few dashes Tabasco sauce, and cook for 10 minutes. Stir in the scallions.

4 Heat the rice according to the package directions, then place a serving in a deep bowl, ladle a serving of the gumbo over the rice, and serve.

Ingredients SERVES 4

8 small chicken pieces, skinned
1 tbsp. olive oil
1 tbsp. unsalted butter
1 onion, peeled and chopped
2–3 garlic cloves, peeled and chopped
1–2 red chiles, seeded and chopped
2 celery stalks, trimmed and sliced
1 red bell pepper, seeded and chopped
$2^1/_4$ cups trimmed okra
4 spicy link sausages
2 tbsp. all-purpose flour
$7^3/_4$ cups chicken stock
few dashes Tabasco sauce
6 scallions, trimmed and chopped
2 9-oz. packages microwaveable
    basmati rice, to serve

Food fact

Gumbos vary from area to area and there are no rules, so the ingredients can vary according to the region and availability of the ingredients.

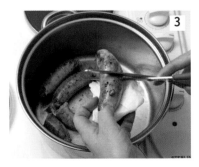

Chicken Basquaise

1 Dry the chicken pieces well with paper towels. Put the flour in a plastic bag, season with salt and pepper, and add the chicken pieces. Twist the bag to seal, then shake to coat the chicken pieces thoroughly.

2 Heat 2 tablespoons of the oil in a large, heavy saucepan over medium-high heat. Add the chicken pieces and cook for about 15 minutes, turning on all sides, until well browned. Using a slotted spoon, transfer to a plate.

3 Add the remaining olive oil to the saucepan, then add the onion and bell peppers. Reduce the heat to medium and cook, stirring frequently, until starting to brown and soften. Stir in the garlic and chorizo and continue cooking for an additional 3 minutes. Add the rice and cook for about 2 minutes, stirring to coat with the oil, until the rice is translucent and golden.

4 Stir in the stock, crushed chiles, thyme, tomato paste, and salt and pepper, and bring to a boil. Return the chicken to the saucepan, pressing it gently into the rice. Cover and cook over very low heat for about 45 minutes until the chicken and rice are cooked and tender.

5 Gently stir in the ham, ripe olives, and half the parsley. Cover and heat for an additional 5 minutes. Sprinkle with the remaining parsley and serve immediately.

Ingredients   SERVES 4–6

3 lb. chicken, cut into 8 pieces
2 tbsp. all-purpose flour
salt and freshly ground black pepper
3 tbsp. olive oil
1 large onion, peeled and sliced
2 red bell peppers, seeded and
    cut into thick strips
2 garlic cloves, peeled and crushed
$^1/_4$ lb. spicy chorizo sausage, cut into
    $^1/_2$-in. pieces
heaping 1 cup long-grain white rice
2 cups chicken stock
1 tsp. crushed dried chiles
$^1/_2$ tsp. dried thyme
1 tbsp. tomato paste
$1^1/_4$ cups diced Spanish ham
12 ripe olives
2 tbsp. freshly chopped parsley

Helpful hint

Look for olives that are already pitted and avoid those that have been marinated in a very spicy marinade, as this could affect the taste of the finished dish.

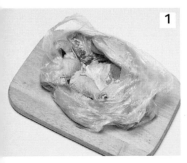

Chicken & Seafood Risotto

1 Heat half the oil in an 18-in. paella pan or deep, wide skillet. Add the chicken pieces and fry for 15 minutes, turning continuously until golden. Remove from the pan and set aside. Add the chorizo and ham to the pan and cook for 6 minutes until crisp, stirring occasionally. Remove and add to the chicken.

2 Add the onion to the pan and cook for 3 minutes, or until beginning to soften. Add the bell peppers and garlic, and cook for 2 minutes; add to the chicken, chorizo, and ham.

3 Add the remaining oil to the pan and stir in the rice until well coated. Stir in the bay leaves, thyme, and saffron, then pour in the wine, and bubble until evaporated. Stir in the stock and bring to a boil, stirring occasionally.

4 Return the chicken, chorizo, ham, and vegetables to the pan, burying them in the rice. Season to taste with salt and pepper. Reduce the heat and simmer for 10 minutes, stirring occasionally.

5 Add the peas and seafood, pushing them gently into the rice. Cover and cook over low heat for 5 minutes, or until the rice and shrimp are tender and the clams and mussels open (discard any that do not open). Let stand for 5 minutes. Sprinkle with the parsley, garnish, and serve.

Ingredients   SERVES 6–8

$^1/_2$ cup olive oil

3 lbs. chicken, cut into 8 pieces

$^3/_4$ lbs. spicy chorizo sausage, cut into
   $^1/_2$-in. pieces

$^2/_3$ cup diced cooked ham

1 onion, peeled and chopped

2 red or yellow bell peppers, seeded and
   cut into 1-in. pieces

4 garlic cloves, peeled and finely chopped

$4^1/_3$ cups short-grain Spanish rice or
   Arborio rice

2 bay leaves

1 tsp. dried thyme

1 tsp. saffron strands, lightly crushed

$^3/_4$ cup dry white wine

$6^1/_2$ cups chicken stock

salt and freshly ground black pepper

$^2/_3$ cup fresh shelled peas

1 lb. uncooked shrimp

36 clams and/or mussels, well scrubbed

2 tbsp. freshly chopped parsley

To garnish:

lemon wedges

fresh parsley sprigs

Chicken & White Wine Risotto

1 Heat the oil and half the butter in a large, heavy saucepan over medium-high heat. Add the shallots and cook for 2 minutes until softened, stirring frequently. Add the rice and cook for 2–3 minutes, stirring frequently, until the rice is translucent and well coated.

2 Pour in half the wine; it will bubble and steam rapidly. Cook, stirring constantly, until the liquid is absorbed. Add a ladleful of the hot stock and cook until the liquid is absorbed. Carefully stir in the chicken.

3 Continue adding the stock, about half a ladleful at a time, allowing each addition to be absorbed before adding the next; never allow the rice to cook dry. This process should take about 20 minutes. The risotto should have a creamy consistency and the rice should be tender but firm to the bite.

4 Stir in the remaining wine and cook for 2–3 minutes. Remove from the heat and stir in the remaining butter with the Parmesan cheese and half the chopped herbs. Season to taste with salt and pepper. Spoon into warmed shallow bowls and sprinkle each with the remaining chopped herbs. Serve immediately.

Ingredients   SERVES 4–6

2 tbsp. olive oil
7 tbsp. butter
2 shallots, peeled and finely chopped
1$^3/_4$ cups Arborio rice
2$^1/_2$ cups dry white wine
3$^1/_4$ cups heated chicken stock
$^3/_4$ lb. skinless chicken breast fillets, thinly sliced
$^1/_2$ cup grated Parmesan cheese
2 tbsp. freshly chopped dill or parsley
salt and freshly ground black pepper

Pad Thai

1 To make the sauce, whisk all the sauce ingredients in a bowl and set aside. Put the rice noodles in a large bowl and pour over enough hot water to cover. Let stand for about 15 minutes until softened. Drain and rinse, then drain again.

2 Heat the oil in a wok over high heat until hot, but not smoking. Add the chicken strips and stir-fry until they begin to color. Using a slotted spoon, transfer to a plate. Reduce the heat to medium-high.

3 Add the shallots, garlic, and scallions, and stir-fry for 1 minute. Stir in the rice noodles, then the sauce; mix well.

4 Add the chicken strips with the crabmeat, bean sprouts, and radish, and stir well. Cook for about 5 minutes, stirring frequently, until heated through. If the noodles begin to stick, add a little water.

5 Turn into a large, shallow serving dish and sprinkle with the chopped peanuts, if desired. Serve immediately.

Ingredients   SERVES 4

$^1/_2$ lb. flat rice noodles

2 tbsp. vegetable oil

$^1/_2$ lb. boneless chicken breast, skinned and thinly sliced

4 shallots, peeled and thinly sliced

2 garlic cloves, peeled and finely chopped

4 scallions, trimmed and diagonally sliced into 2-in. pieces

$^3/_4$ lb. fresh white crabmeat or tiny shrimp

$1^1/_2$ cups rinsed and drained fresh bean sprouts

2 tbsp. preserved or fresh radish, chopped

2–3 tbsp. roasted peanuts, chopped (optional)

For the sauce:

3 tbsp. Thai fish sauce

2–3 tbsp. rice vinegar or cider vinegar

1 tbsp. oyster sauce

1 tbsp. toasted sesame oil

1 tbsp. light brown sugar

1 red chile, seeded and thinly sliced

Persian Chicken Pilaf

1 Heat the oil in a large, heavy saucepan over medium-high heat. Cook the chicken pieces in batches until lightly browned. Return all the browned chicken to the saucepan.

2 Add the onions to the saucepan, reduce the heat to medium, and cook for 3–5 minutes, stirring frequently, until the onions begin to soften. Add the cumin and rice and stir to coat the rice. Cook for about 2 minutes until the rice is golden and translucent. Stir in the tomato paste and the saffron strands, then season to taste with salt and pepper.

3 Add the pomegranate juice and stock and bring to a boil, stirring once or twice. Add the apricots and raisins and stir gently. Reduce the heat to low and cook for 30 minutes until the chicken and rice are tender and the liquid is absorbed.

4 Turn into a shallow serving dish and sprinkle with the chopped mint or parsley. Serve immediately, garnished with pomegranate seeds, if desired.

Ingredients   SERVES 6

2–3 tbsp. vegetable oil

1$^1/_2$ lb. boneless, skinless chicken pieces (breast and thighs), cut into 1-in. pieces

2 medium onions, peeled and coarsely chopped

1 tsp. ground cumin

heaping 1 cup long-grain white rice

1 tbsp. tomato paste

1 tsp. saffron strands

salt and freshly ground black pepper

1 cup pomegranate juice

3$^3/_4$ cups chicken stock

1 cup halved, pitted dried apricots or dried plums (prunes)

2 tbsp. raisins

2 tbsp. freshly chopped mint or parsley

pomegranate seeds, to garnish (optional)

Creamy Chicken & Rice Pilaf

1 Heat the butter in a large, deep skillet over medium-high heat. Add the almonds and pistachios and cook for about 2 minutes, stirring constantly, until golden. Using a slotted spoon, transfer to a plate.

2 Add the chicken pieces to the pan and cook for 5 minutes, or until golden, turning once. Remove from the pan and set aside. Add the oil to the pan. Cook the onions for 10 minutes, or until golden, stirring frequently. Stir in the garlic, ginger, and spices, and cook for 2–3 minutes, stirring.

3 Add 2–3 tablespoons of the yogurt and cook, stirring, until the moisture evaporates. Continue adding the yogurt in this way until it is used up.

4 Return the chicken and nuts to the pan and stir. Stir in $^1/_2$ cup boiling water and season to taste with salt and pepper. Cook, covered, over low heat for 10 minutes until the chicken is tender. Stir in the cream, grapes, and half the herbs. Gently fold in the rice. Heat for 5 minutes, sprinkle with the remaining herbs, then serve.

Ingredients   SERVES 4

4 tbsp. butter
1 cup flaked almonds
$^2/_3$ cup unsalted, shelled pistachio nuts
4–6 skinless chicken breast fillets, each
     cut into 4 pieces
2 tbsp. vegetable oil
2 medium onions, peeled and
     thinly sliced
2 garlic cloves, peeled and
     finely chopped
1-in. piece fresh ginger, finely chopped
6 green cardamom pods, lightly crushed
4–6 whole cloves
2 bay leaves
1 tsp. ground coriander
$^1/_2$ tsp. cayenne pepper, or to taste
1 cup plain yogurt
salt and freshly ground black pepper
1 cup heavy cream
$^1/_2$ lb. seedless green grapes,
     halved if large
2 tbsp. freshly chopped cilantro or mint
$2^1/_4$ cups cooked white basmati rice

Turkey Cutlets Marsala with Wilted Watercress

1 Place each turkey cutlet between two sheets of nonstick parchment paper, and, using a meat mallet or rolling pin, pound to make a cutlet about $1/8$ inch thick. Put the flour in a shallow dish, add the thyme, season to taste with salt and pepper, and stir to blend. Coat each cutlet lightly on both sides with the flour mixture, then set aside.

2 Heat half the olive oil in a large skillet, then add the watercress and stir-fry for about 2 minutes until just wilted and brightly colored. Season with salt and pepper. Using a slotted spoon, transfer the watercress to a plate and keep warm.

3 Add half the butter to the skillet, and, when melted, add the mushrooms. Stir-fry for 4 minutes, or until golden and tender. Remove from the skillet and set aside. Add the remaining butter to the skillet and, working in batches, cook the flour-coated cutlets for 2–3 minutes on each side until golden and cooked thoroughly, using the remaining oil if necessary. Remove from the skillet and keep warm. Add the Marsala wine to the skillet and stir, scraping up any browned bits from the bottom. Add the stock or water and bring to a boil over high heat. Season lightly. Return the cutlets and mushrooms to the skillet and reheat gently until piping hot. Divide the warm watercress among four serving plates. Arrange one cutlet over each serving of watercress and spoon over the mushrooms and Marsala sauce. Serve immediately.

Ingredients SERVES 4

4 turkey cutlets, $1/4$ lb. each
$1/4$ cup all-purpose flour
$1/2$ tsp. dried thyme
salt and freshly ground black pepper
2 tbsp. olive oil
$2^1/2$ cups watercress
3 tbsp. butter
2 cups wiped and
    quartered mushrooms
$1/4$ cup dry Marsala or Italian
    fortified wine
$1/4$ cup chicken stock or water

Helpful hint

Turkey cutlets are thin slices of turkey breast fillets, which have been flattened. If they are unavailable, substitute chicken breasts that have been halved horizontally and flattened between pieces of plastic wrap.

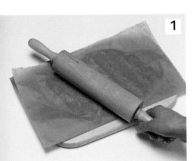

Herbed Hasselback Potatoes with Roasted Chicken

1 Preheat the oven to 400°F. Place a chopstick on either side of a potato, and, with a sharp knife, cut down through the potato until you reach the chopsticks; be careful not to cut right through the potato. Repeat these cuts every $^1/_4$ in. along the length of the potato. Carefully ease 2–4 of the slices apart and slip in a few rosemary sprigs. Repeat with the remaining potatoes. Brush with the oil and season well with salt and pepper.

2 Place the seasoned potatoes in a large roasting pan. Add the parsnips, carrots, and leeks to the potatoes, and cover with a wire rack or trivet.

3 Beat the butter and lemon zest together and season to taste. Smear the chicken with the lemon butter and place on the rack over the vegetables.

4 Roast in the preheated oven for 1 hour 40 minutes, basting the chicken and vegetables occasionally, until cooked thoroughly. The juices should run clear when the thigh is pierced with a skewer. Place the cooked chicken on a warmed serving platter, arrange the roasted vegetables around it, and serve immediately.

Ingredients   SERVES 4–6

8 medium, evenly-sized
  potatoes, peeled
3 large fresh rosemary sprigs
1 tbsp. olive oil
salt and freshly ground black pepper
$^3/_4$ lb. baby parsnips, peeled
$^3/_4$ lb. baby carrots, peeled
$^3/_4$ lb. baby leeks, trimmed
4 tbsp. butter
finely grated zest of 1 lemon,
  preferably unwaxed
$3^1/_2$ lb. chicken

Food fact

Hasselback potatoes were named after the Stockholm restaurant of the same name. Using chopsticks is a great way of ensuring that you slice just far enough through the potatoes so that they fan out during cooking. The potatoes can be given an attractive golden finish by mixing $^1/_4$ tsp. ground turmeric or paprika with the oil.

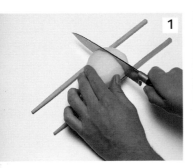

Braised Chicken in Beer

1 Preheat the oven to 375°F. Cut each chicken joint in half and put in an ovenproof casserole dish with the dried plums and bay leaves. To peel the shallots, put in a small bowl and cover with boiling water. After 2 minutes, drain the shallots and rinse under cold water until cool enough to handle. The skins should then peel away easily from the shallots.

2 Heat the oil in a large, nonstick skillet. Add the shallots and cook gently for about 5 minutes until beginning to brown. Add the mushrooms to the skillet and cook for an additional 3–4 minutes until both the mushrooms and shallots are softened.

3 Sprinkle the sugar over the shallots and mushrooms, then add the mustard, tomato paste, beer, and chicken stock. Season to taste with salt and pepper and bring to a boil, stirring to combine. Carefully pour over the chicken.

4 Cover the casserole and cook in the preheated oven for 1 hour. Blend the cornstarch with the lemon juice and 1 tablespoon cold water and stir into the chicken casserole.

5 Return to the oven for 10 minutes, or until the chicken is cooked and the vegetables are tender. Remove the bay leaves and stir in the chopped parsley. Garnish with the Italian parsley. Serve with the mashed potatoes and fresh green vegetables.

Ingredients   SERVES 4

4 chicken joints, skinned
$^2/_3$ cup pitted dried plums
2 bay leaves
12 shallots
2 tsp. olive oil
$1^3/_4$ cups wiped small
    button mushrooms
1 tsp. dark brown sugar
$^1/_2$ tsp. mustard
2 tsp. tomato paste
$^2/_3$ cup light beer
$^2/_3$ cup chicken stock
salt and freshly ground black pepper
2 tsp. cornstarch
2 tsp. lemon juice
2 tbsp. freshly chopped parsley
Italian parsley, to garnish

Chicken Baked in a Salt Crust

1 Preheat the oven to 375°F. Remove the giblets if necessary, and rinse the chicken with cold water. Sprinkle the inside with salt and pepper. Put the onion inside, along with the rosemary, thyme, and bay leaf.

2 Mix the butter, garlic, paprika, and lemon zest together. Starting at the neck end, gently ease the skin from the chicken and push the mixture underneath.

3 To make the salt crust, put the flour and salts in a large bowl and stir together. Make a well in the center. Pour in 2 cups cold water and the oil. Mix to a stiff dough, then knead on a lightly floured surface for 2–3 minutes. Roll out the dough to a 20-inch circle. Place the chicken breast-side down in the center. Lightly brush the edges with water, then fold over to enclose. Pinch the joints together to seal.

4 Put the chicken joint-side down in a roasting pan and cook in the preheated oven for 2³/₄ hours. Remove from the oven and let stand for 20 minutes.

5 Break open the hard crust and remove the chicken. Discard the crust. Remove the skin from the chicken and garnish with the fresh herbs and lemon slices. Serve the chicken immediately.

Ingredients   SERVES 6

4-lb. oven-ready chicken
salt and freshly ground black pepper
1 medium onion, peeled
fresh rosemary sprig
fresh thyme sprig
1 bay leaf
1 tbsp. butter, softened
1 garlic clove, peeled and crushed
pinch paprika
2 tsp. finely grated lemon zest

For the salt crust:

8 cups all-purpose flour
3²/₃ cups fine cooking salt
3²/₃ cups coarse sea salt
2 tbsp. olive oil

To garnish:

fresh herbs
lemon slices

Helpful hint

It is best to avoid eating the skin from the chicken. It is high in fat and also absorbs a lot of salt from the crust.

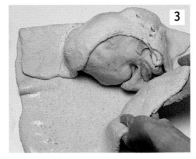

Slow-Roasted Chicken with Potatoes & Oregano

1 Preheat the oven to 375°F. Rinse the chicken and dry well, inside and out, with paper towels. Rub the chicken all over with the lemon halves, then squeeze the juice over it and into the cavity. Put the squeezed halves into the cavity with the quartered onion. Rub the softened butter all over the chicken, and season to taste with salt and pepper, then put it in a large roasting pan, breast-side down. Toss the potatoes in the oil, season with salt and pepper to taste, and add the oregano and fresh thyme. Arrange the potatoes, along with the oil, around the chicken, and carefully pour $^2/_3$ cup water into one end of the pan (not over the oil).

2 Roast in the preheated oven for 25 minutes. Turn the chicken breast-side up. Turn the potatoes, sprinkle with half the fresh herbs, and baste the chicken and potatoes with the juices. Continue roasting for 1 hour, or until the chicken is thoroughly cooked, basting occasionally. If the liquid evaporates completely, add a little more water. The chicken is cooked when the juices run clear when the thigh is pierced with a skewer. Transfer the chicken to a carving dish and let rest for 5 minutes, covered with aluminum foil. Meanwhile, return the potatoes to the oven. Carve the chicken into serving pieces and arrange on a large, heatproof serving dish. Arrange the potatoes around the chicken and drizzle over any remaining juices. Sprinkle with the remaining herbs and serve.

Ingredients   SERVES 6

3–4 lb. oven-ready chicken
1 lemon, halved
1 onion, peeled and quartered
4 tbsp. butter, softened
salt and freshly ground black pepper
2¹/₄ lb. potatoes, peeled
    and quartered
3–4 tbsp. extra virgin olive oil
1 tbsp. dried oregano, crumbled
1 tsp. fresh thyme leaves
2 tbsp. freshly chopped thyme
fresh sage leaves, to garnish

Helpful hint

When testing if the chicken is cooked, use a clean, long skewer, because this will reach the very center of the thigh.

Turkey Hash with Potato & Beets

1 In a large, heavy skillet, heat the oil and half the butter over medium heat until sizzling. Add the bacon and cook for 4 minutes, or until crisp and golden, stirring occasionally. Using a slotted spoon, transfer to a large bowl. Add the onion to the pan and cook for 3–4 minutes until soft and golden, stirring frequently.

2 Meanwhile, add the turkey, potatoes, parsley, and flour to the cooked bacon in the bowl. Stir and toss gently, then fold in the diced beets.

3 Add half the remaining butter to the skillet and then the turkey-vegetable mixture. Stir, then spread the mixture to evenly cover the bottom of the pan. Cook for 15 minutes, or until the underside is crisp and brown, pressing the hash firmly with a spatula. Remove from the heat.

4 Place a large plate over the skillet and, holding the plate and pan together with an oven mitt, invert the hash out onto the plate. Heat the remaining butter in the pan, slide the hash back into the pan, and cook for 4 minutes, or until crisp and brown on the other side. Invert onto the plate again and serve immediately with a green salad.

Ingredients   SERVES 4

2 tbsp. vegetable oil
4 tbsp. butter
4 slices bacon, diced or sliced
1 medium onion, peeled and
   finely chopped
2¼ cups diced, cooked turkey
2½ cups finely chopped
   cooked potatoes
2–3 tbsp. freshly chopped parsley
2 tbsp. all-purpose flour
1¾ cups diced, cooked beets
green salad, to serve

Tasty tip

A hash is usually made just with potatoes, but here they are combined with ruby red beets, which add vibrant color and a sweet, earthy flavor to the dish. Make sure that you buy plain beets rather than the pickled variety.

Sweet & Sour Rice with Chicken

1 Trim the scallions, then cut lengthwise into fine strips. Drop into a large bowl of ice-cold water and set aside.

2 Mix together the sesame oil and Chinese five-spice powder and use to rub into the cubed chicken. Heat the wok, then add the oil, and, when hot, cook the garlic and onion for 2–3 minutes until transparent and softened.

3 Add the chicken and stir-fry over medium-high heat until the chicken is golden and cooked through. Using a slotted spoon, remove from the wok and keep warm.

4 Stir the rice into the wok and add the water, ketchup, tomato paste, honey, vinegar, and soy sauce. Stir well to mix. Bring to a boil, then simmer until almost all of the liquid is absorbed. Stir in the carrot and chicken, and continue to cook for 3–4 minutes. Drain the scallions, which will have become curly. Garnish with the scallion curls and serve immediately with the rice and chicken.

Ingredients SERVES 4

4 scallions

2 tsp. sesame oil

1 tsp. Chinese five-spice powder

1 lb. chicken breast, cut into cubes

1 tbsp. vegetable oil

1 garlic clove, peeled and crushed

1 medium onion, peeled and sliced
   into thin wedges

$1^{1}/_{3}$ cups long-grain white rice

$2^{1}/_{2}$ cups water

4 tbsp. ketchup

1 tbsp. tomato paste

2 tbsp. honey

1 tbsp. vinegar

1 tbsp. dark soy sauce

1 carrot, peeled and thinly sliced

Food fact

Five-spice powder is a mixture of finely ground star anise, fennel, cinnamon, cloves and Sichuan pepper, and adds a unique sweet and spicy aniseed flavor to food.

Chinese-Style Fried Rice

1 Heat a wok or large, deep skillet until very hot, add the oil, and heat for 30 seconds. Add the onions and stir-fry for 2 minutes. Stir in the garlic and ginger and cook for 1 minute. Add the cooked chicken and ham and stir-fry for an additional 2–3 minutes.

2 Add the rice, water chestnuts, and shrimp, if using, with 2 tablespoons water, and stir-fry for 2 minutes until the rice is heated through.

3 Beat the eggs with 1 teaspoon of the sesame oil and season to taste with salt and pepper. Make a well in the center of the rice, then pour in the egg mixture and stir immediately, gradually drawing the rice mixture into the egg until the egg is cooked.

4 Add the scallions, soy and chili sauces, cilantro, and a little water, if necessary. Adjust the seasoning and drizzle with the remaining sesame oil. Sprinkle with the nuts, decorate with the cilantro sprig and serve.

Ingredients   SERVES 4–6

2–3 tbsp. peanut oil or vegetable oil
2 small onions, peeled and
  cut into wedges
2 garlic cloves, peeled and thinly sliced
1-in. piece fresh ginger, peeled and
  cut into thin slivers
$2^1/_2$ cups shredded, cooked chicken
$1^1/_4$ cups shredded, cooked ham
$1^1/_3$ cups cooked and cooled long-grain
  white rice
$^1/_2$ cup sliced canned water chestnuts
$1^1/_2$ cups cooked, peeled shrimp (optional)
3 extra-large eggs
3 tsp. sesame oil
salt and freshly ground black pepper
6 scallions, trimmed and sliced into
  $^1/_2$-in. pieces
2 tbsp. dark soy sauce
1 tbsp. sweet chili sauce
2 tbsp. freshly chopped cilantro

To garnish:
2 tbsp. chopped roasted peanuts
fresh cilantro sprig

Shredded Duck in Lettuce Leaves

1 Cover the dried shiitake mushrooms with almost-boiling water, leave for 20 minutes, then drain and slice thinly.

2 Heat a large wok, add the oil, and, when hot, stir-fry the duck for 3–4 minutes until sealed. Remove with a slotted spoon and set aside. Add the chili, scallions, garlic, and shiitake mushrooms to the wok, and stir-fry for 2–3 minutes until softened.

3 Add the bean sprouts, the soy sauce, Chinese rice wine or dry sherry, and honey or brown sugar to the wok, and continue to stir-fry for 1 minute, or until blended. Stir in the duck and stir-fry for 2 minutes, or until well mixed together and heated all the way through. Transfer to a heated serving dish.

4 Arrange the hoisin sauce in a small bowl on a tray or plate with a pile of lettuce leaves and the mint leaves. Let each guest spoon a little hoisin sauce onto a lettuce leaf, then top with a large spoonful of the stir-fried duck and vegetables, and roll up the leaf to enclose the filling. Serve with the dipping sauce.

Ingredients   SERVES 4–6

2 tbsp. dried shiitake mushrooms
2 tbsp. vegetable oil
1 lb. boneless, skinless duck breast,
    cut crosswise into thin strips
1 red chile, seeded and thinly
    sliced diagonally
4–6 scallions, trimmed and
    diagonally sliced
2 garlic cloves, peeled and crushed
$^3/_4$ cup bean sprouts
3 tbsp. soy sauce
1 tbsp. Chinese rice wine or dry sherry
1–2 tsp. honey or brown sugar
4–6 tbsp. hoisin or plum sauce

To serve:

large, crisp lettuce leaves, such
    as romaine
handful fresh mint leaves
plum sauce or sweet chili sauce,
    for dipping

Thai Chicken Fried Rice

1 Using a sharp knife, trim the chicken, discarding any sinew or fat, and cut into small cubes. Set aside.

2 Heat a wok or large skillet, add the oil, and, when hot, add the garlic and cook for 10–20 seconds until just golden. Add the curry paste and stir-fry for a few seconds. Add the chicken and stir-fry for 3–4 minutes until tender and the chicken has turned white.

3 Stir the cold cooked rice into the chicken mixture, then add the soy sauce, fish sauce, and sugar, stirring well after each addition. Stir-fry for 2–3 minutes until the chicken is cooked through and the rice is piping hot.

4 Check the seasoning and, if necessary, add a little extra soy sauce. Turn the rice-and-chicken mixture into a warmed serving dish. Season lightly with black pepper and garnish with shredded scallions and onion slices. Serve immediately.

Ingredients   SERVES 4

6 oz. boneless chicken breast

2 tbsp. vegetable oil

2 garlic cloves, peeled and
  finely chopped

2 tsp. medium curry paste

3 cups cold cooked rice

1 tbsp. light soy sauce

2 tbsp. Thai fish sauce

large pinch sugar

freshly ground black pepper

To garnish:

2 scallions, trimmed and
  shredded lengthwise

$1/2$ small onion, peeled and very
  finely sliced

Helpful hint

Store cooked rice in the refrigerator overnight in a bowl with a tight-fitting lid or plastic wrap.

Chicken Chow Mein

1 Place the egg noodles in a large bowl and cover with boiling water. Leave for 3–5 minutes, drain, and add 1 tablespoon of the sesame oil, and stir lightly. Set aside.

2 Place 2 teaspoons of the light soy sauce, 1 tablespoon of the Chinese rice wine or sherry, 1 teaspoon of the sesame oil, and salt and pepper to taste in a bowl. Add the chicken and stir well. Cover lightly and allow to marinate in the refrigerator for about 15 minutes.

3 Heat the wok over high heat, add 1 tablespoon of the peanut oil, and, when very hot, add the chicken and its marinade, and stir-fry for 2 minutes. Remove the chicken and juices and set aside. Wipe the wok clean with absorbent paper towels.

4 Reheat the wok and add the remaining oil. Add the garlic and toss in the oil for 20 seconds. Add the snow peas and the ham and stir-fry for 1 minute. Add the noodles, the remaining light soy sauce, Chinese rice wine or sherry, the dark soy sauce, and sugar. Season to taste with salt and pepper and stir-fry for 2 minutes.

5 Add the chicken and juices to the wok and stir-fry for 4 minutes, or until the chicken is cooked. Drizzle with the remaining sesame oil. Garnish with scallions and sesame seeds, then serve.

Ingredients   SERVES 4

$3^{1}/_{4}$ cups fine egg noodles

5 tsp. sesame oil

4 tsp. light soy sauce

2 tbsp. Chinese rice wine or dry sherry

salt and freshly ground black pepper

$^{1}/_{2}$ lb. skinless chicken breast fillets,
  cut into strips

3 tbsp. peanut oil

2 garlic cloves, peeled and
  finely chopped

$^{1}/_{2}$ cup finely sliced snow peas

$^{1}/_{2}$ cup fine strips cooked ham

2 tsp. dark soy sauce

pinch sugar

To garnish:

shredded scallions

toasted sesame seeds

Food fact

Sesame oil is a thick, rich, golden brown oil made from toasted sesame seeds. It is used in Chinese cooking, mainly as a seasoning.

Noodles with Turkey & Mushrooms

1 Place the noodles in a large bowl and cover with boiling water. Leave for 3–5 minutes, then drain and set aside.

2 Heat the wok, add the oil, and, when hot, add the onion and stir-fry for 1 minute. Add the ginger and garlic and stir-fry for an additional 3 minutes, then add the turkey strips and stir-fry for 4–5 minutes until sealed and golden brown.

3 Wipe and slice the wild or cremini mushrooms into similar-sized pieces and add to the wok with the button mushrooms. Stir-fry for 3–4 minutes until tender. When all the vegetables are tender and the turkey is cooked, add the soy sauce, hoisin sauce, sherry, and vegetable stock.

4 Mix the cornstarch with 2 tablespoons water and add to the wok, then cook, stirring, until the sauce thickens. Add the drained noodles to the wok, cook, stirring for 2–3 minutes until the noodles are hot, then serve immediately.

Ingredients SERVES 4

$3^{1}/_{4}$ cups dried fine egg noodles

1 tbsp. peanut oil

1 red onion, peeled and sliced

2 tbsp. freshly grated ginger

3 garlic cloves, peeled and finely chopped

$^{3}/_{4}$ lb. turkey breast, skinned and cut into strips

$1^{1}/_{4}$ cups assorted wild or cremini mushrooms

1 cup baby button mushrooms

2 tbsp. dark soy sauce

2 tbsp. hoisin or plum sauce

2 tbsp. dry sherry

4 tbsp. vegetable stock

2 tsp. cornstarch

Chicken & Red Pepper Curried Rice

1   Lightly beat the egg white with the salt and 2 teaspoons of the cornstarch until smooth. Add the chicken and mix together well. Cover and chill in the refrigerator for 20 minutes.

2   Heat a wok and, when hot, add 1 tablespoon of the oil and heat for 30 seconds. Add the chicken mixture to the wok and stir-fry for 2–3 minutes until the chicken has turned white all over. Using a slotted spoon, lift the cubes of chicken from the wok, then drain on paper towels.

3   Add the remaining oil to the wok, heat for 30 seconds, then add the red bell pepper and stir-fry for 1 minute over high heat. Add the curry powder and cook for 30 seconds, then add the chicken stock, sugar, Chinese rice wine, and soy sauce.

4   Mix the remaining cornstarch with 1 teaspoon cold water and add to the wok, stirring. Bring to a boil and simmer gently for 1 minute.

5   Return the chicken to the wok, then simmer for an additional minute before adding the rice. Stir over medium heat for another 2 minutes until heated through. Garnish with the sprigs of cilantro, and serve.

Ingredients   SERVES 4

1 extra-large egg white
1 tsp. salt
1 tbsp. cornstarch
$3/4$ lb. skinless chicken breast fillets, cut into chunks
2 tbsp. peanut oil
1 red bell pepper, seeded and coarsely chopped
1 tbsp. curry powder or paste
$1/2$ cup chicken stock
1 tsp. sugar
1 tbsp. Chinese rice wine or dry sherry
1 tbsp. light soy sauce
$2 1/4$ cups cold cooked long-grain white rice
fresh cilantro sprigs, to garnish

Helpful hint

Other ingredients can be added to this dish. Try zucchini cut into thin batons, coarsely grated carrot and halved baby corns.

Chicken with Noodles

1 If having to use dried noodles, cook the noodles according to the package directions. Drain and rinse under cold water. Drain again and set aside.

2 Slice the chicken into fine shreds and mix with 2 teaspoons of the light soy sauce and the Chinese rice wine. Allow to marinate in the refrigerator for 10 minutes.

3 Heat a wok, add 2 teaspoons of the oil, and, when hot, stir-fry the chicken shreds for about 2 minutes, then transfer to a plate. Wipe the wok clean with absorbent paper towels.

4 Return the wok to the heat and add the remaining oil. Add the garlic, then, after 10 seconds, add the snow peas and bacon. Stir-fry for an additional minute, then add the remaining soy sauce, sugar, and scallions. Stir-fry for an additional 2 minutes, then add the chicken.

5 Add the drained noodles or the ready-to-wok to the wok, stir-fry for an additional 3–4 minutes until the chicken is cooked through and the noodles are hot. Add the sesame oil and mix together. Serve either hot or cold.

Ingredients   SERVES 2–3

if available, 2 5-oz. packages straight-to-wok egg noodles, or $3^1/_4$ cups medium dried egg noodles

$^1/_4$ lb. boneless, skinless chicken breast fillets

1 tbsp. light soy sauce

2 tsp. Chinese rice wine or dry sherry

5 tsp. peanut oil

2 garlic cloves, peeled and finely chopped

$^1/_2$ cup snow peas

2 tbsp. bacon, cut into fine strips

$^1/_2$ tsp. sugar

2 scallions, peeled and finely chopped

1 tsp. sesame oil

Food fact

Chow mein literally means 'stir-fried noodles.' There are no hard and fast rules about which meat, fish or vegetables can be used. Chow mein also makes a tasty salad if served cold.

Chicken Wraps

1 Slice the chicken across the grain into ³/₄-inch-wide strips. Place in a bowl with the lime zest, lime juice, sugar, oregano, cinnamon, and cayenne pepper. Mix well and marinate while making the tortillas.

2 Sift the flour, salt, and baking powder into a bowl. Rub in the shortening, then sprinkle with 4 tablespoons warm water and mix to a stiff dough. Knead on a lightly floured surface for 10 minutes until smooth and elastic. Divide the dough into 12 equal pieces and roll out each to a 6-inch circle. Cover with plastic wrap to prevent them from drying out before cooking.

3 Heat a nonstick wok or large skillet and cook each tortilla for about 1 minute on each side, or until golden and slightly blistered. Remove the tortillas and keep warm and pliable in a dish towel.

4 Heat 2 tablespoons of the oil in the wok and stir-fry the onions for 5 minutes until lightly browned. Remove with a slotted spoon and set aside. Add the remaining oil to the wok. Drain the chicken from the marinade and add it to the wok. Stir-fry for 5 minutes, then return the onions, add the bell pepper slices, and cook for an additional 3–4 minutes until the chicken is cooked through and the vegetables are tender. Season to taste with salt and pepper and serve immediately with the tortillas, sour cream, and guacamole.

Ingredients   SERVES 4

For the stir-fried chicken:

4 skinless chicken breast fillets
2 tsp. finely grated lime zest
1 tbsp. lime juice
1 tbsp. sugar
2 tsp. dried oregano
¹/₂ tsp. ground cinnamon
¹/₄ tsp. cayenne pepper
3 tbsp. corn oil
2 onions, peeled and sliced
1 green, 1 red, and 1 yellow bell pepper, seeded and sliced
salt and freshly ground black pepper

For the tortillas:

2¹/₄ cups all-purpose flour
pinch salt
¹/₄ tsp. baking powder
¹/₄ cup vegetable shortening

To serve:

sour cream
guacamole

Fish & Seafood

If you love seafood, whether it's Tuna Chowder or Smoked Haddock Rösti, this is the section to stir up something scrumptious. If you're hoping for heat, Thai Hot & Sour Shrimp Soup or Spicy Cod Rice will not be found lacking. If hot's a not, there's something for everyone, from Pea & Shrimp Risotto to restaurant favorites such as Bouillabaisse.

Thai Shellfish Soup

1 Peel the shrimp. Using a sharp knife, remove the black vein along the back of the shrimp. Pat dry with paper towels and set aside. Skin the fish, pat dry, and cut into 1-in. chunks. Place in a bowl with the shrimp and the squid. Sprinkle with the lime juice and set aside.

2 Scrub the mussels, removing their beards and any barnacles. Discard any mussels that are open, damaged, or do not close when tapped. Place in a large saucepan and add ²/₃ cup of the coconut milk.

3 Cover, bring to a boil, then simmer for 5 minutes, or until the mussels open, shaking the saucepan occasionally. Lift out the mussels, discarding any unopened ones, strain the liquid through a cheesecloth-lined strainer, and set aside.

4 Rinse and dry the saucepan. Heat the peanut oil, add the curry paste, and cook for 1 minute, stirring all the time. Add the lemongrass, lime leaves, fish sauce, the strained mussel liquid, and the remaining coconut milk. Bring the contents of the saucepan to a very gentle simmer. Add the fish mixture to the saucepan and simmer for 2–3 minutes until just cooked. Stir in the mussels, with or without their shells, as preferred. Season to taste with salt and pepper, then garnish with cilantro. Ladle into warmed bowls and serve immediately.

Ingredients   SERVES 4–6

³/₄ lb. shrimp
³/₄ lb. firm, white fish, such
   as monkfish
6 oz. small squid
1 tbsp. lime juice
1 lb. mussels
2 cups coconut milk
1 tbsp. peanut oil
2 tbsp. Thai red curry paste
1 lemongrass stalk, bruised
3 kaffir lime leaves, finely shredded
2 tbsp. Thai fish sauce
salt and freshly ground black pepper
fresh cilantro, to garnish

Food fact
Squeezing lime juice on top of seafood improves its texture, as the acid in the juice firms up the flesh.

Thai Hot & Sour Shrimp Soup

1 Remove the heads from the shrimp by twisting away from the body, and set aside. Shell the shrimp, leaving the tails on, and set aside the shells with the heads. Using a sharp knife, remove the black vein from the back of the shrimp. Rinse and dry the shrimp and set aside. Rinse and dry the heads and shells.

2 Heat a wok, add the oil, and, when hot, add the shrimp heads and shells, the lemongrass, ginger, garlic, cilantro stems, and black pepper, and stir-fry for 2–3 minutes until the shrimp heads and shells turn pink and all the ingredients are colored.

3 Carefully add the water to the wok and return to a boil, skimming off any scum that rises to the surface. Simmer over a medium heat for 10 minutes, or until slightly reduced. Strain through a fine strainer and return the clear shrimp stock to the wok.

4 Bring the stock back to a boil and add the shrimp, chiles, lime leaves, and scallions, and simmer for 3 minutes, or until the shrimp turn pink. Season with the fish sauce and lime juice. Spoon into heated soup bowls, dividing the shrimp evenly, and sprinkle a few cilantro leaves over the surface.

Ingredients SERVES 6

$1^{1}/_{2}$ lb. large shrimp

2 tbsp. vegetable oil

3–4 lemongrass stalks, coarsely chopped and outer leaves discarded

1-in. piece fresh ginger, peeled and finely chopped

2–3 garlic cloves, peeled and crushed

small bunch fresh cilantro, leaves stripped and set aside, stems finely chopped

$^{1}/_{2}$ tsp. freshly ground black pepper

6 cups water

1–2 small red chiles, seeded and thinly sliced

1–2 small green chiles, seeded and thinly sliced

6 kaffir lime leaves, thinly shredded

4 scallions, trimmed and diagonally sliced

1–2 tbsp. Thai fish sauce

1–2 tbsp. freshly squeezed lime juice

Food fact

Thai fish sauce, made from fermented anchovies, has a sour, salty, fishy flavor.

Corn & Crab Soup

1 Wash and dry the corn cobs. Using a sharp knife and holding the corncobs at an angle to the cutting board, cut down along the cobs to remove the kernels, then scrape the cobs to remove any excess milky residue. Put the kernels and the milky residue into a large wok.

2 Add the chicken stock to the wok and place over high heat. Bring to a boil, stirring and pressing some of the kernels against the side of the wok to squeeze out the starch to help thicken the soup. Simmer for 15 minutes, stirring occasionally.

3 Add the scallions, ginger, sherry or Chinese rice wine, soy sauce, and brown sugar to the wok, and season to taste with salt and pepper. Simmer for an additional 5 minutes, stirring occasionally.

4 Blend the cornstarch with 1 tablespoon cold water to form a smooth paste and mix into the soup. Return to a boil, then simmer over medium heat until thickened.

5 Add the crabmeat, stirring until blended. Beat the egg white with the sesame oil and stir into the soup in a slow, steady stream, stirring continuously. Stir in the chopped cilantro and serve immediately.

Ingredients SERVES 4

1 lb. fresh corn on the cob

5 cups chicken stock

2–3 scallions, trimmed and finely chopped

$1/_2$-in. piece fresh ginger, peeled and finely chopped

1 tbsp. dry sherry or Chinese rice wine

2–3 tsp. soy sauce

1 tsp. light brown sugar

salt and freshly ground black pepper

2 tsp. cornstarch

$1/_2$ lb. white crabmeat, fresh or canned

1 large egg white

1 tsp. sesame oil

1–2 tbsp. freshly chopped cilantro

Helpful hint

If fresh crab is unavailable, use thawed frozen or drained canned crabmeat. Alternatively, use a mixture of fresh shellfish.

Shrimp & Chile Soup

1   To make the scallion curls, finely shred the scallions lengthwise. Place in a bowl of ice-cold water and set aside. Remove the heads and shells from the shrimp, leaving the tails intact.

2   Split the shrimp almost in two to form a butterfly shape, and individually remove the black vein that runs down the back of each.

3   In a large saucepan, heat the stock with the lime zest and juice, fish sauce, chile, and soy sauce. Bruise the lemongrass by crushing it along its length with a rolling pin, then add to the stock mixture.

4   When the stock mixture is boiling, add the shrimp and cook until they are pink. Remove the lemongrass and add the rice vinegar and cilantro. Spoon into bowls and garnish with the scallion curls. Serve immediately.

Ingredients   SERVES 4

2 scallions, trimmed
8 oz. whole, jumbo shrimp
3 cups fish stock
2 tsp. finely grated lime zest
1 tbsp. lime juice
1 tbsp. fish sauce
1 red chile, seeded and chopped
1 tbsp. soy sauce
1 lemongrass stalk
2 tbsp. rice vinegar
4 tbsp. freshly chopped cilantro

Tasty tip

For a more substantial dish, cook $1/4$ cup Thai fragrant rice for 12–15 minutes until just cooked. Drain, then place a little in the soup bowl and spoon the prepared soup on top.

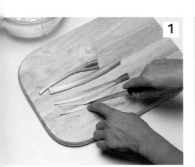

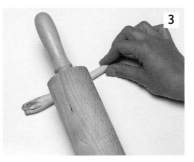

Mediterranean Chowder

1 Heat the oil and butter together in a large saucepan. Add the onion, celery, and garlic, and cook gently for 2–3 minutes until softened. Add the chile and stir in the flour. Cook, stirring, for an additional minute.

2 Add the potatoes to the saucepan with the stock. Bring to a boil, cover, and simmer for 10 minutes. Add the fish cubes to the saucepan with the chopped parsley and cook for an additional 5–10 minutes until the fish and potatoes are just tender.

3 Stir in the peeled shrimp and corn kernels and season to taste with salt and pepper. Pour in the cream and adjust the seasoning if necessary.

4 Sprinkle the chives over the chowder. Ladle into six large bowls and serve immediately, with plenty of warm, crusty bread.

Ingredients SERVES 6

1 tbsp. olive oil
1 tbsp. butter
1 large onion, peeled and
   finely sliced
4 celery stalks, trimmed and
   thinly sliced
2 garlic cloves, peeled and crushed
1 Thai chile, seeded and
   finely chopped
1 tbsp. all-purpose flour
$1\frac{1}{3}$ cups peeled and diced potatoes
$2\frac{1}{2}$ cups fish or vegetable stock
$1\frac{1}{2}$ lb. white fish fillet, cut into
   1-in. cubes
2 tbsp. freshly chopped parsley
$\frac{3}{4}$ cup large, peeled, cooked shrimp
7 oz. canned corn kernels, drained
salt and freshly ground black pepper
$\frac{2}{3}$ cup light cream
1 tbsp. freshly cut chives
warm, crusty bread, to serve

Tuna Chowder

1 Heat the oil in a large, heavy saucepan. Add the onion and celery and cook gently for about 5 minutes, stirring from time to time until the onion is softened.

2 Stir in the flour and cook for about 1 minute to thicken. Take the saucepan off the heat and gradually pour in the milk, stirring throughout.

3 Add the tuna and its liquid, the drained corn, and the freshly chopped thyme. Mix gently, then bring to a boil. Cover with a lid and simmer for 5 minutes

4 Remove the saucepan from the heat and season to taste with salt and pepper. Sprinkle the chowder with the cayenne pepper and chopped parsley. Divide among soup bowls and serve immediately.

Ingredients   SERVES 4

2 tsp. oil

1 onion, peeled and finely chopped

2 celery stalks, trimmed and
    finely sliced

1 tbsp. all-purpose flour

$2^1/_2$ cups milk

7 oz. canned tuna in water

11 oz. canned of corn, drained

2 tsp. freshly chopped thyme

salt and freshly ground black pepper

pinch of cayenne pepper

2 tbsp. freshly chopped parsley

Tasty tip

This creamy soup also works well using equivalent amounts of canned crabmeat instead of the tuna. For a contrasting taste and to enhance the delicate creaminess of this soup, add a spoonful of crème fraîche to the top of the soup. Sprinkle with cayenne pepper and then garnish with a few long chives.

Smoked Haddock Soup

1 Melt the butter in a large, heavy saucepan, add the onion, and sauté for 3 minutes, stirring occasionally. Add the bay leaf and stir, then sprinkle in the flour and cook over low heat for 2 minutes, stirring frequently. Add the potatoes.

2 Take off the heat and gradually stir in the milk and water. Return to the heat and bring to a boil, stirring. Reduce the heat to a simmer and cook for 10 minutes.

3 Meanwhile, discard any pin bones from the fish and cut into small pieces. Add to the pan together with the corn and peas. Cover and cook gently, stirring occasionally, for 10 minutes, or until the vegetables and fish are cooked.

4 Add pepper and nutmeg to taste, then stir in the cream and heat gently for 1–2 minutes until piping hot. Sprinkle with the parsley and serve with crusty bread.

Ingredients   SERVES 4

2 tbsp. unsalted butter
1 onion, peeled and chopped
1 fresh bay leaf
3 tbsp. plus 1 tsp. all-purpose flour
12 oz. new potatoes, scrubbed and
    cut into small pieces
generous $2^1/_2$ cups low-fat milk
$1^1/_4$ cups water
12 oz. undyed smoked haddock
    fillet, skinned
$^1/_2$ cup frozen corn kernels
$^1/_3$ cup frozen peas
freshly ground black pepper
$^1/_2$ tsp. freshly grated nutmeg
2–3 tbsp. light cream
2 tbsp. freshly chopped parsley
crusty bread, to serve

Tasty tip
Add 4 oz peeled shrimp with the cream, if liked. Be careful not to overcook, or the shrimp will lose their flavor and will be tough.

Bouillabaisse

1 Cut the fish into thick pieces, peel the shrimp if necessary, and rinse well. Place the saffron strands in a small bowl, cover with warm water, and let stand to steep for at least 10 minutes.

2 Heat the oil in a large, heavy saucepan or casserole dish, add the onions and celery, and sauté for 5 minutes, stirring occasionally. Add the tomatoes, bay leaf, garlic, and bouquet garni, and stir until lightly coated with the oil.

3 Place the firm fish on top of the tomatoes and pour in the saffron-steeped water and enough water to just cover. Bring to a boil, reduce the heat, cover with a lid, and cook for 8 minutes.

4 Add the soft-flesh fish and continue to simmer for 5 minutes, or until all the fish are cooked. Season to taste with salt and pepper, remove and discard the bouquet garni, and serve with French bread.

Ingredients   SERVES 4–6

$1\frac{1}{2}$ lb. assorted fish, such as whiting, mackerel, red mullet, salmon, and jumbo shrimp, cleaned and skinned

few saffron strands

3 tbsp. olive oil

2 onions, peeled and sliced

2 celery stalks, trimmed and sliced

$1\frac{1}{4}$ cups peeled and chopped ripe tomatoes

1 fresh bay leaf

2–3 garlic cloves, peeled and crushed

1 bouquet garni

sea salt and freshly ground black pepper

French bread, to serve

Tasty tip

Traditionally, eight different fish are used for this dish. Use as many as you wish, but make sure you remove as many bones as possible and use fresh not smoked fish.

Roasted Monkfish with Vegetables

1 Preheat the oven to 375°F. Cut all the root vegetables, including the onions, into even wedges and place in a large roasting pan. Reserve 2 garlic cloves and add the remainder to the roasting pan. Season to taste with salt and pepper and pour over 1 tablespoon of the oil. Turn the vegetables over until lightly coated in the oil, then roast in the oven for 20 minutes.

2 Meanwhile, cut the monkfish tails into fillets. Using a sharp knife, cut down both sides of the central bone to form 2 fillets from each tail. Discard any skin or membrane, then rinse thoroughly. Make small incisions down the length of the monkfish fillets.

3 Cut the reserved garlic cloves into small slivers and break the rosemary into small sprigs. Insert the garlic and rosemary into the incisions in the fish.

4 Cut the bell peppers into strips, then add to the roasting pan together with the cherry tomatoes. Place the fish on top and drizzle with the remaining oil. Cook for an additional 12–15 minutes until the vegetables and fish are thoroughly cooked. Serve sprinkled with chopped parsley.

Ingredients   SERVES 4

3 medium parsnips, peeled
2 medium sweet potatoes, peeled
4 medium carrots, peeled
2 onions, peeled
4–6 garlic cloves, peeled
salt and freshly ground black pepper
2 tbsp. olive oil
2 small monkfish tails
    (about 2 lb.) or 4 monkfish fillets
    (about 1½ lb.)
2–3 fresh rosemary sprigs
2 yellow bell peppers, seeded
12 cherry tomatoes
2 tbsp. freshly chopped parsley

Helpful hint

Other fish can be cooked in this way. If using whole fish, prepare as above, but wrap in nonstick parchment paper. If using other fillets, check the cooking time, as most fillets will take slightly less time than the monkfish fillets.

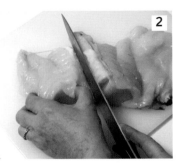

Mediterranean Fish Stew

1   Heat the olive oil in a large saucepan. Add the onion, garlic, fennel, and celery, and cook over low heat for 15 minutes, stirring frequently, until the vegetables are soft and just beginning to turn brown.

2   Add the canned tomatoes with their juice, the oregano, bay leaf, orange zest, orange juice, and saffron strands. Bring to a boil, reduce the heat, and simmer for 5 minutes. Add the fish stock and vermouth and season to taste with salt and pepper. Bring to a boil. Reduce the heat and simmer for 20 minutes.

3   Wipe or rinse the haddock and sea bass fillets and remove as many of the bones as possible. Place on a cutting board and cut into 2-inch cubes. Add to the saucepan and cook for 3 minutes. Add the shrimp and cook for an additional 5 minutes. Adjust the seasoning to taste and serve with crusty bread.

Ingredients
SERVES 4–6

4 tbsp. olive oil
1 onion, peeled and finely sliced
5 garlic cloves, peeled and finely sliced
1 fennel bulb, trimmed and
    finely chopped
3 celery stalks, trimmed and
    finely chopped
14 oz. canned chopped tomatoes
1 tbsp. freshly chopped oregano
1 bay leaf
1 tbsp. orange zest
3 tbsp. orange juice
1 tsp. saffron strands
3 cups fish stock
3 tbsp. dry vermouth
salt and freshly ground black pepper
$^1/_2$ lb. thick haddock fillets
$^1/_2$ lb. sea bass fillets
2 cups shelled jumbo shrimp
crusty bread, to serve

Chunky Fish Casserole

1 Melt the butter or margarine in a large saucepan, add the onions and bell pepper, and cook for 5 minutes, or until softened. Cut the peeled potatoes into 1-inch cubes, rinse lightly, and shake dry, then add them to the onions and bell pepper in the saucepan. Add the zucchini and cook, stirring frequently, for an additional 2–3 minutes.

2 Sprinkle the flour, paprika, and vegetable oil into the saucepan and cook, stirring continuously, for 1 minute. Pour in $^2/_3$ cup of the wine with all the stock and the chopped tomatoes, and bring to a boil.

3 Add the basil to the casserole, season to taste with salt and pepper, and cover. Simmer for 15 minutes, then add the fish and the remaining wine, and simmer gently for an additional 5–7 minutes until the fish and vegetables are just tender. Garnish with basil sprigs and serve immediately with freshly cooked rice.

Ingredients   SERVES 6

4 tbsp. butter or margarine
2 large onions, peeled and
    sliced into rings
1 red bell pepper, seeded and
    roughly chopped
1 lb. potatoes, peeled
4 cups thickly sliced zucchini
2 tbsp. all-purpose flour
1 tbsp. paprika
2 tsp. vegetable oil
$1^1/_4$ cups white wine
$^2/_3$ cup fish stock
14 oz. canned chopped tomatoes
2 tbsp. freshly chopped basil
salt and freshly ground black pepper
1 lb. firm white fish fillet, skinned and
    cut into 1-in. cubes
fresh basil sprigs, to garnish
freshly cooked rice, to serve

Thai Green Fragrant Mussels

1 Scrub the mussels under cold running water, removing any barnacles and beards. Discard any that have broken or damaged shells, or are opened and do not close when tapped gently.

2 Heat a wok or large skillet, add the oil, and, when hot, add the mussels. Shake gently and cook for 1 minute, then add the garlic, ginger, sliced lemongrass, chiles, green bell pepper, scallions, 2 tablespoons of the chopped cilantro, and the sesame oil.

3 Stir-fry over medium heat for 3–4 minutes until the mussels are cooked and have opened. Discard any mussels that remain unopened.

4 Pour the lime juice and coconut milk into the wok and bring to a boil. Tip the mussels and the cooking liquid into warmed individual bowls. Sprinkle with the remaining chopped cilantro and serve immediately with crusty bread.

Ingredients · SERVES 4

$4^1/_2$ lb. fresh mussels

4 tbsp. olive oil

2 garlic cloves, peeled and finely sliced

3 tbsp. ginger, peeled and finely sliced

3 lemongrass stalks, outer leaves discarded and finely sliced

1–3 red or green chiles, seeded and chopped

1 green bell pepper, seeded and diced

5 scallions, trimmed and finely sliced

3 tbsp. freshly chopped cilantro

1 tbsp. sesame oil

juice of 3 limes

14 oz. canned coconut milk

crusty bread, to serve

Mussels Arrabbiata

1   Clean the mussels by scrubbing with a small, soft brush, removing the beard and any barnacles from the shells. Discard any mussels that are open or have damaged shells. Place in a large bowl and cover with cold water. Change the water frequently before cooking, and leave in the refrigerator until needed.

2   Heat the olive oil in a large saucepan and fry the onion, garlic, and chile until soft but not colored. Add the tomatoes and bring to a boil, then simmer for 15 minutes.

3   Add the white wine to the tomato sauce, bring the sauce to a boil, and add the mussels. Cover and carefully shake the saucepan. Cook the mussels for 5–7 minutes until the shells have opened.

4   Add the olives to the saucepan and cook uncovered for about 5 minutes to warm through. Season to taste with salt and pepper and sprinkle over the chopped parsley. Discard any mussels that have not opened, and serve immediately with lots of crusty bread.

Ingredients   SERVES 4

4 lb. mussels
3–4 tbsp. olive oil
1 large onion, peeled and sliced
4 garlic cloves, peeled and
   finely chopped
1 red chile, seeded and
   finely chopped
$1^3/_4$ lb. (28 oz.) canned
   chopped tomatoes
$^2/_3$ cup white wine
1 cup halved and pitted ripe olives
salt and freshly ground black pepper
2 tbsp. freshly chopped parsley
crusty bread, to serve

Food fact

Arrabbiata sauce is a classic Italian tomato-based sauce, usually containing onions, bell peppers, garlic, and fresh herbs. It needs slow simmering to bring out the flavor and is excellent with meat, poultry, and pasta, as well as seafood.

Seafood Risotto

1 Melt the butter in a large, heavy saucepan, add the shallots
and garlic, and cook for 2 minutes until slightly softened. Add
the rice and cook for 1–2 minutes, stirring continuously, then
pour in the wine and boil for 1 minute.

2 Pour in half the hot stock, bring to a boil, cover the saucepan,
and simmer gently for 15 minutes, adding the remaining
stock a little at a time. Continue to simmer for 5 minutes, or
until the rice is cooked and all the liquid is absorbed.

3 Meanwhile, prepare the seafood by peeling the shrimp and
removing their heads and tails. Drain the clams and discard
the liquid. Cut the smoked salmon into thin strips.

4 When the rice is cooked, stir in the shrimp, clams, smoked
salmon strips, and half the chopped parsley, then heat for
1–2 minutes until everything is piping hot. Turn into a serving
dish, sprinkle with the remaining parsley and serve
immediately with a green salad and crusty bread.

Ingredients   SERVES 4

4 tbsp. butter
2 shallots, peeled and finely chopped
1 garlic clove, peeled and crushed
2 cups Arborio rice
$^2/_3$ cup white wine
$2^1/_2$ cups fish or vegetable
   stock, heated
$^3/_4$ cup whole cooked, unpeeled,
   large shrimp
10 oz. canned baby clams
$^1/_3$ cup smoked salmon trimmings
2 tbsp. freshly chopped parsley

To serve:

green salad
crusty bread

Smoked Haddock Rösti

1. Dry the grated potatoes in a clean dish towel. Rinse the grated onion thoroughly in cold water, dry in a clean dish towel, and add to the potatoes.

2. Stir the garlic into the potato mixture. Skin the smoked haddock and remove as many of the tiny pin bones as possible. Cut into thin slices and set aside.

3. Heat the oil in a large, nonstick skillet. Add half the potatoes and press down in the skillet. Season to taste with salt and pepper.

4. Add a layer of fish and a sprinkling of lemon zest, parsley, and a little black pepper.

5. Top with the remaining potatoes and press down firmly. Cover with a sheet of foil and cook on the lowest heat for 25–30 minutes.

6. Preheat the broiler 2–3 minutes before the end of the cooking time. Remove the foil and place the rösti under the broiler to brown. Turn out onto a warmed serving dish and serve immediately with spoonfuls of sour cream, lemon wedges, and mixed lettuce leaves.

Ingredients   SERVES 4

1 lb. potatoes, peeled and
   coarsely grated
1 large onion, peeled and
   coarsely grated
2–3 garlic cloves, peeled
   and crushed
1 lb. smoked haddock
1 tbsp. olive oil
salt and freshly ground black pepper
2 tsp. finely grated lemon zest
1 tbsp. freshly chopped parsley
2 tbsp. low-fat sour cream
lemon wedges, to serve
lettuce leaves, to serve

Helpful hint

These delicious fish rösti are best if they are prepared, cooked, and then eaten right away.

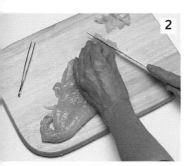

Paella

1 Rinse the mussels under cold running water, scrubbing well to remove any grit and barnacles, then pull off the hairy "beards." Tap any open mussels sharply with a knife, and discard if they refuse to close. Place in a large bowl and cover with cold water. Change the water frequently before cooking and leave in the refrigerator until required.

2 Heat the oil in a paella pan or large, heavy skillet and gently cook the chicken thighs for 10–15 minutes until golden. Remove and keep warm.

3 Fry the onion and garlic in the remaining oil in the pan for 2–3 minutes, then add the tomatoes, bell peppers, peas, and paprika, and cook for an additional 3 minutes. Add the rice to the pan and return the chicken with the turmeric and half the stock. Bring to a boil and simmer, gradually adding more stock as it is absorbed. Cook for 20 minutes, or until most of the stock has been absorbed and the rice is almost tender.

4 Add the mussels to the pan, pressing them gently into the rice. Cook for 5 minutes, then discard any that have not opened. Stir the shrimp into the rice. Season to taste with salt and pepper. Heat for 2–3 minutes until piping hot. Squeeze the juice from one of the limes over the paella. Cut the remaining lime and the lemon into wedges and arrange on top of the paella. Sprinkle with the basil, garnish with the shrimp, and serve.

Ingredients SERVES 6

1 lb. fresh mussels
4 tbsp. olive oil
6 medium chicken thighs
1 medium onion, peeled and finely chopped
1 garlic clove, peeled and crushed
$^3/_4$ cup skinned, seeded, and chopped tomatoes
1 red bell pepper, seeded, and chopped
1 green bell pepper, seeded and chopped
$^2/_3$ cup frozen peas
1 tsp. paprika
$2^2/_3$ cups Arborio rice
$^1/_2$ tsp. turmeric
$3^3/_4$ cups chicken stock, warmed
1 cup peeled large shrimp
salt and freshly ground black pepper
2 limes
1 lemon
1 tbsp. freshly chopped basil
whole, cooked, unpeeled shrimp, to garnish

Spanish Omelet with Smoked Fish

1 Fill a large, nonstick, heavy skillet with water (enough to cover the fish) and bring to a boil. Turn off the heat, lower the fish into the water, season with salt and pepper, and leave for 5 minutes. Drain, set aside the fish and let cool. When cool, discard the skin and any pin bones and cut into small pieces.

2 Dry the pan, add the oil and heat. Add the potatoes, onions, and garlic, and cook gently for 10–15 minutes until golden brown, then add the red bell pepper. Scatter the fish on top of the vegetables and cook for 3 minutes.

3 When the vegetables are cooked, drain off any excess oil. Beat the butter and cream into the eggs, then stir in the parsley. Pour the egg mixture over the top of the vegetables and fish and cook gently for 5 minutes, or until the eggs become firm.

4 Sprinkle the shredded cheese over the top and place the pan under a preheated broiler. Cook for 2–3 minutes until the cheese is golden and bubbling. Carefully slide the omelet onto a large plate, and serve immediately with plenty of bread and salad.

Ingredients   SERVES 3–4

$^1/_4$ lb. smoked haddock
salt and freshly ground black pepper
3 tbsp. sunflower oil
2 cups peeled and diced potatoes
2 medium onions, peeled and cut
    into wedges
2–4 large garlic cloves, peeled and
    thinly sliced
1 large red bell pepper, seeded,
    quartered, and thinly sliced
2 tbsp. butter, melted
1 tbsp. heavy cream
6 large eggs, beaten
2 tbsp. freshly chopped
    Italian parsley
$^1/_2$ cup shredded cheddar cheese

To serve:
crusty bread
tossed green salad

Pea & Shrimp Risotto

1 Peel the shrimp and set aside the heads and shells. Remove the black vein from the back of each shrimp, then wash and dry on absorbent paper towels and set aside.

2 Melt half the butter in a saucepan, add the shrimp heads and shells, and fry, stirring occasionally, for 3–4 minutes until golden. Strain the butter, discard the heads and shells, and return the butter to the pan.

3 Add 2 tablespoons of the butter to the pan and stir-fry the shrimp for 3–4 minutes. Remove from the pan and set aside.

4 Melt the remaining butter in the pan and fry the onion and garlic for 5 minutes until softened, but not browned. Add the rice and stir the grains in the butter for 1 minute, until they are coated thoroughly. Add the white wine and boil rapidly until the wine is reduced by half.

5 Add the heated stock to the rice, a ladleful at a time. Stir continuously, adding the stock as it is absorbed, until the rice is creamy, but still has a bite in the center.

6 Stir the cooked shrimp into the rice, along with the peas. Add the chopped mint and season to taste with salt and pepper. Cover the pan and let the shrimp infuse for 5 minutes before serving.

Ingredients   SERVES 6

1 lb. whole shrimp
7 tbsp. butter
1 red onion, peeled and chopped
4 garlic cloves, peeled and
   finely chopped
1 cup risotto rice
$^2/_3$ cup dry white wine
5 cups vegetable or fish
   stock, heated
3 cups frozen peas, thawed
4 tbsp. freshly chopped mint
salt and freshly ground black pepper

Tasty tip

Cooking the shrimp shells and heads before cooking the dish adds a great deal of flavor to the rice. Alternatively, the shells and heads could be added to the stock and simmered for 10 minutes. Strain the stock, pressing the shells and heads well to extract the maximum flavor.

Spicy Cod Rice

1 Mix together the flour, cilantro, cumin, and ground coriander on a large plate. Coat the cod in the spice mixture, then place on a baking tray, cover, and chill in the refrigerator for 30 minutes.

2 Heat a large wok, then add 2 tablespoons of the oil and heat until almost smoking. Stir-fry the cashews for 1 minute until brown, then remove and set aside.

3 Add an additional tablespoon of the oil and heat until almost smoking. Add the cod and stir-fry for 2 minutes. Using a spatula, turn the cod pieces over and cook for an additional 2 minutes until golden. Transfer to a warmed plate, cover, and keep warm.

4 Add the remaining oil to the wok, heat until almost smoking, then stir-fry the scallions and chile for 1 minute before adding the carrot and peas, and stir-frying for an additional 2 minutes. Stir in the rice, chili sauce, soy sauce, and cashews, and stir-fry for an additional 3 minutes. Add the cod, heat for 1 minute, then serve immediately.

Ingredients   SERVES 4

1 tbsp. all-purpose flour

1 tbsp. freshly chopped cilantro

1 tsp. ground cumin

1 tsp. ground coriander

$1\frac{1}{4}$-lb. thick-cut cod fillet, skinned
  and cut into large chunks

4 tbsp. peanut oil

$\frac{1}{2}$ cup cashews

1 bunch scallions, trimmed and
  diagonally sliced

1 red chile, seeded and chopped

1 carrot, peeled and cut
  into thin strips

1 cup frozen peas

5 cups cooked long-grain rice

2 tbsp. sweet chili sauce

2 tbsp. soy sauce

Helpful hint

Care is needed when frying nuts, as they have a tendency to burn very quickly. An alternative is to toast them on a baking tray in the oven at 350° F for about 5 minutes until they are golden and fragrant.

Singapore Noodles

1 Put the noodles into a large bowl and add enough boiling water to cover. Let stand for 3 minutes, or until slightly underdone according to the package directions. Drain well and set aside.

2 Heat a wok until almost smoking. Add the oil and carefully swirl to coat the sides of the wok. Add the shallots, garlic, and ginger, and cook for a few seconds. Add the bell pepper and chili, and stir-fry for 3–4 minutes until the pepper has softened.

3 Add the shrimp, pork, chicken, and curry powder to the wok. Stir-fry for an additional 4–5 minutes until the meat and shrimp are colored on all sides, then add the fennel seeds and the cinnamon and stir to mix.

4 Add the drained noodles to the wok along with the peas, and cook for an additional 1–2 minutes until heated through. Add the lemon juice to taste. Sprinkle with the fresh cilantro leaves and serve immediately.

Ingredients   SERVES 4

$2^2/_3$ cups flat rice noodles

3 tbsp. corn oil

2 shallots, peeled and sliced

2 garlic cloves, peeled and crushed

2 tbsp. freshly grated ginger

1 red bell pepper, seeded and
    finely sliced

1 hot red chile, seeded and
    finely chopped

$1^1/_2$ cups shelled shrimp

$1^1/_4$ cups boneless pork, diced

2 cups boneless chicken, diced

1 tbsp. curry powder

1 tsp. each crushed fennel seeds and
    ground cinnamon

$^1/_2$ cup thawed frozen peas

3 tbsp. lemon juice

3 tbsp. fresh cilantro leaves

Helpful hint

This is a great dish for using up leftover meat. If using cooked meat, reduce the cooking time accordingly, but make sure that it is piping hot.

Vegetables

Anyone who ever complained of vegetables being flat and flavorless will find themselves singing a different tune after tasting this tongue-tantalizing section. From succulent soups such as Carrot & Ginger to choice curries such as Pumpkin & Chickpea, the vegetable will be the most in-demand item on your kitchen's menu.

Potato & Fennel Soup

1 Melt the butter in a large, heavy saucepan. Add the onions with the garlic and half the salt, and cook over medium heat, stirring occasionally, for 7–10 minutes until the onions are very soft and beginning to turn brown.

2 Add the potatoes, fennel, caraway seeds, and the remaining salt. Cook for about 5 minutes, then pour in the vegetable stock. Bring to a boil, partially cover, and simmer for 15–20 minutes until the potatoes are tender. Stir in the chopped parsley and adjust the seasoning to taste.

3 For a smooth-textured soup, let cool slightly, then pour into a food processor or blender and blend until smooth. Reheat the soup gently, then ladle into individual soup bowls. For a chunky soup, omit this blending stage and ladle straight from the saucepan into soup bowls.

4 Swirl a spoonful of crème fraîche into each bowl and serve immediately with coarsely torn pieces of French bread.

Ingredients   SERVES 4

2 tbsp. butter
2 large onions, peeled and thinly sliced
2–3 garlic cloves, peeled and crushed
1 tsp. salt
2 medium potatoes (about
    1 lb.), peeled and diced
1 fennel bulb, trimmed and
    finely chopped
$^1/_2$ tsp. caraway seeds
$4^1/_4$ cups vegetable stock
2 tbsp. freshly chopped parsley
freshly ground black pepper
4 tbsp. crème fraîche or Greek yogurt
coarsely torn French bread, to serve

Food fact

Fennel has a distinct aniseed flavor, which mellows and sweetens when cooked. Look out for well-rounded bulbs with bright green fronds. Fennel is at its best when fresh, so should be used as soon as possible after buying. It may be stored in the salad drawer of the refrigerator for a few days.

Potato, Leek & Rosemary Soup

1 Melt the butter in a large saucepan, add the leeks, and cook gently for 5 minutes, stirring frequently. Remove 1 tablespoon of the cooked leeks and set aside for garnishing.

2 Add the potatoes, vegetable stock, rosemary sprigs, and milk. Bring to a boil, then reduce the heat, cover, and simmer gently for 20–25 minutes until the vegetables are tender.

3 Cool for 10 minutes. Discard the rosemary, then pour into a food processor or blender and blend well to form a smooth-textured soup.

4 Return the soup to the cleaned saucepan and stir in the chopped parsley and crème fraîche. Season to taste with salt and pepper. If the soup is too thick, stir in a little more milk or water. Reheat gently, without boiling, then ladle into warmed soup bowls. Garnish the soup with the set-aside leeks and serve immediately with whole-wheat rolls.

Ingredients   SERVES 4–6

2 tbsp. butter
1 lb. leeks, trimmed and finely sliced
4 cups peeled and coarsely
   chopped potatoes
3³/₄ cups vegetable stock
4 fresh rosemary sprigs
2 cups whole milk
2 tbsp. freshly chopped parsley
2 tbsp. crème fraîche
salt and freshly ground black pepper
whole-wheat rolls, to serve

Tasty tip

This rosemary-scented version of potato and leek soup is equally delicious served cold, when it would be called Vichyssoise. Allow the soup to cool before covering, then chill in the refrigerator for at least 2 hours. The soup will thicken as it chills, so you may need to thin it to the desired consistency with more milk or stock and season before serving.

Bread & Tomato Soup

1 Make a small cross in the base of each tomato, then place in a bowl and cover with boiling water. Allow to stand for 2 minutes, or until the skins have started to peel away, then drain, remove the skins and seeds, and chop into large pieces.

2 Heat 3 tablespoons of the olive oil in a saucepan and gently cook the onion until softened. Add the peeled tomatoes, chopped basil, garlic, and chili powder. Season to taste with salt and pepper. Pour in the stock, cover the saucepan, bring to a boil, and simmer gently for 15–20 minutes.

3 Remove the crusts from the bread and break into small pieces. Remove the tomato mixture from the heat and stir in the bread. Cover and allow to stand for 10 minutes, or until the bread has blended with the tomatoes. Season to taste. Serve the soup warm or cold with a swirl of olive oil on the top, garnished with a spoonful of diced cucumber and basil leaves.

Ingredients   SERVES 4

6 medium, very ripe tomatoes
$1/4$ cup olive oil
1 onion, peeled and finely chopped
1 tbsp. freshly chopped basil
3 garlic cloves, peeled and crushed
$1/4$ tsp. hot chili powder
salt and freshly ground black pepper
$2^{1}/_{2}$ cups chicken stock
6 slices stale white bread
$1/4$ small cucumber, cut into
  small dice
4 whole basil leaves

Tasty tip

This soup is best made when fresh tomatoes are in season. If you want to make it at other times of the year, replace the fresh tomatoes with $1^{3}/_{4}$ lb. (28 oz.) canned peeled plum tomatoes—Italian, if possible. You may need to cook the soup for 5–10 minutes longer.

Rice & Tomato Soup

1 Preheat the oven to 425°F. Rinse and drain the basmati rice. Place the canned tomatoes with their juice in a large, heavy saucepan with the garlic, lime zest, oil, and sugar. Season to taste with salt and pepper. Bring to a boil, then reduce the heat, cover, and simmer for 10 minutes.

2 Add the vegetable stock or water and the rice and bring to a boil, stirring frequently. Reduce the heat to a simmer and cook, uncovered, for an additional 15–20 minutes until the rice is tender. If the soup is too thick, add a little more water. Set aside and keep warm if the croutons are not ready.

3 Meanwhile, to make the croutons, mix the pesto and olive oil together in a large bowl. Add the bread cubes and toss until they are coated completely with the mixture. Spread on a baking sheet and bake in the preheated oven for 10–15 minutes until golden and crisp, turning them over halfway through cooking. Serve the soup immediately, sprinkled with the warm croutons.

Ingredients

SERVES 4

heaping $^3/_4$ cup easy-cook
   basmati rice
14 oz. canned chopped tomatoes
2 garlic cloves, peeled and crushed
grated zest of $^1/_2$ lime
2 tbsp. extra virgin olive oil
1 tsp. sugar
salt and freshly ground black pepper
$1^3/_4$ cups vegetable stock or water

For the croutons:
2 tbsp. prepared pesto sauce
2 tbsp. olive oil
6 thin slices ciabatta bread, cut into
   $^1/_2$-in. cubes

Helpful hint
If time is short or facilities limited, and for a more accurately one-pot meal, look out in your local supermarket or grocery store for ready-made croutons. There is now a wide variety of different flavors available.

Lettuce Soup

1 Bring a large saucepan of water to a boil and blanch the lettuce leaves for 3 minutes. Drain and dry thoroughly on absorbent paper towels, then shred with a sharp knife.

2 Heat the oil and butter in a clean saucepan, add the lettuce, scallions, and parsley, and cook together for 3–4 minutes until very soft.

3 Stir in the flour and cook for 1 minute, then gradually pour in the stock, stirring throughout. Bring to a boil and season to taste with salt and pepper. Reduce the heat, cover, and simmer gently for 10–15 minutes until soft.

4 Allow the soup to cool slightly, then either strain or puree in a blender. Alternatively, leave the soup chunky. Stir in the cream, add more seasoning, if desired, then add the cayenne pepper.

5 Arrange the slices of ciabatta bread in a large soup dish or in individual bowls and pour the soup over the bread. Garnish with sprigs of parsley and serve immediately.

Ingredients   SERVES 4

2 heads iceberg lettuce, quartered,
   with hard core removed
1 tbsp. olive oil
4 tbsp. butter
$^1/_2$ cup trimmed and
   chopped scallions
1 tbsp. freshly chopped parsley
1 tbsp. all-purpose flour
$2^1/_2$ cups chicken stock
salt and freshly ground black pepper
$^2/_3$ cup light cream
$^1/_4$ tsp. cayenne pepper, or to taste
thick slices stale ciabatta bread
parsley sprigs, to garnish

Helpful hint

Do not prepare the lettuce too far in advance. Iceberg lettuce has a tendency to discolor when sliced, which may in turn discolor the soup.

Cream of Pumpkin Soup

1 Cut the pumpkin flesh into 1-inch cubes. Heat the olive oil in a large saucepan and cook the pumpkin for 2–3 minutes, coating it completely with oil. Chop the onion and leek finely, and dice the carrot and celery stalks.

2 Add the vegetables to the saucepan with the garlic and cook, stirring, for 5 minutes, or until they have begun to soften. Cover the vegetables with the water and bring to a boil. Season with plenty of salt and pepper, and the grated nutmeg, then cover and simmer for 15–20 minutes until all of the vegetables are tender.

3 When the vegetables are tender, remove from the heat, cool slightly, then pour into a food processor or blender. Blend to form a smooth paste, then pass through a strainer into a clean saucepan.

4 Adjust the seasoning to taste and add all but 2 tablespoons of the cream and enough water to obtain the correct consistency. Bring the soup to boiling point, add the cayenne pepper, and serve immediately swirled with cream and accompanied by warm herb bread.

Ingredients SERVES 6–8

2 lb. pumpkin flesh, seeds discarded
$1/4$ cup olive oil
1 large onion, peeled
1 leek, trimmed
1 carrot, peeled
2 celery stalks
4 garlic cloves, peeled and crushed
6 cups water
salt and freshly ground black pepper
$1/4$ tsp. freshly grated nutmeg
$2/3$ cup light cream
$1/4$ tsp. cayenne pepper
warm herb bread, to serve

Tasty tip

If you cannot find pumpkin, try replacing it with squash. Butternut, acorn, or turban squash would all make suitable substitutes. Avoid spaghetti squash, which is not firm-fleshed when cooked.

Carrot & Ginger Soup

1 Preheat the oven to 350°F. Coarsely chop the bread. Dissolve the yeast extract in 2 tablespoons warm water and mix with the bread.

2 Spread the bread cubes over a lightly greased baking sheet and cook for 20 minutes, turning halfway through. Remove from the oven and set aside.

3 Heat the oil in a large saucepan. Gently cook the onion and garlic for 3–4 minutes. Stir in the ground ginger and cook for 1 minute to release the flavor.

4 Add the chopped carrots, then stir in the stock and the fresh ginger. Simmer gently for 15 minutes.

5 Remove from the heat and allow to cool slightly. Blend until smooth, then season to taste with salt and pepper. Stir in the lemon juice. Garnish with the chives and lemon zest, and serve immediately.

Ingredients SERVES 4

4 slices bread, crusts removed
1 tsp. yeast extract
2 tsp. olive oil
1 onion, peeled and chopped
1 garlic clove, peeled and crushed
$\frac{1}{2}$ tsp. ground ginger
$2\frac{1}{2}$ cups peeled and chopped carrots
4 cups vegetable stock
1-in. piece fresh ginger, peeled and finely grated
salt and freshly ground black pepper
1 tbsp. lemon juice

To garnish:
chives
lemon zest

Vegetable & Lentil Casserole

1   Preheat the oven to 325°F. Pour the lentils out onto a plate and look through them for any small stones, then rinse the lentils and set aside.

2   Heat the oil in a large, flameproof casserole dish (or a deep skillet, if preferred), add the onion, garlic, carrots, and celery, and sauté for 5 minutes, stirring occasionally.

3   Add the squash and lentils. Pour in the stock and season to taste with salt and pepper. Add the oregano sprigs and bring to a boil.

4   If a skillet has been used, transfer the vegetable-and-stock mixture to a casserole dish. Cover with a lid and cook in the oven for 25 minutes.

5   Remove the casserole dish from the oven, add the red bell pepper and zucchini, and stir. Return the casserole dish to the oven and cook for an additional 20 minutes, or until all the vegetables are tender. Adjust the seasoning, garnish with sprigs of oregano, and serve with sour cream on the side.

Ingredients   SERVES 4

heaping 1 cup French green lentils
1–2 tbsp. olive oil
1 onion, peeled and chopped
2–3 garlic cloves, peeled and crushed
$2^1/_2$ cups chunkily chopped carrot
3 celery stalks, trimmed and sliced
$2^2/_3$ cups diced butternut squash
$4^1/_3$ cups vegetable stock
salt and freshly ground black pepper
few fresh oregano sprigs, plus extra
   to garnish
1 large red bell pepper, seeded
   and chopped
2 zucchini, trimmed and sliced
scant $^2/_3$ cup sour cream, to serve

Tasty tip

Other vegetables can be added to the casserole, such as sweet potato, eggplant, turnips, or parsnips.

Three Bean Tagine

1   Place warm water into a small bowl and sprinkle with saffron strands. Let stand to steep for at least 10 minutes.

2   Heat the oil in a large, heavy saucepan, add the eggplant and onion, and sauté for 5 minutes before adding the sweet potatoes, carrots, cinnamon stick, and ground cumin. Cook, stirring, until the vegetables are lightly coated in the cumin. Add the saffron with the soaking liquid and season to taste with salt and pepper. Pour in the stock and add the mint sprigs.

3   Rinse the beans, add to the pan, and bring to a boil. Reduce the heat, cover with a lid, and simmer for 20 minutes. Add the apricots and cook, stirring occasionally, for an additional 10 minutes, or until the vegetables are tender. Adjust the seasoning to taste, then serve sprinkled with chopped mint.

Ingredients   SERVES 4

few saffron strands
2–3 tbsp. olive oil
1 small eggplant, trimmed and diced
1 onion, peeled and chopped
$2^2/_3$ cups diced sweet potatoes
$1^1/_2$ cups chopped carrots
1 cinnamon stick, bruised
$1^1/_2$ tsp. ground cumin
salt and freshly ground black pepper
$2^1/_2$ cups vegetable stock
2 fresh mint sprigs
7 oz. canned red kidney
   beans, drained
11 oz. canned haricot
   beans, drained
11 oz. canned flageolet
   beans, drained
1 cup chopped dried apricots
1 tbsp. freshly chopped mint,
   to garnish

Fragrant Vegetable Pot

1 Heat the oil in a large wok or heavy saucepan and add the spices, including the chile. Cook for 2 minutes, stirring continuously.

2 Add the rice and stir until lightly coated in the spices and oil. Pour in half the stock, bring to a boil, and cook for 10 minutes.

3 Add the remaining stock, the broccoli, green beans, and chopped bell peppers, and cook for an additional 10 minutes. Add the sugar snap peas and baby corn and cook for 5–8 minutes until the vegetables are tender. Remove and discard the cinnamon stick and star anise and serve sprinkled with chopped cilantro, if using.

Ingredients SERVES 4

1 tbsp. peanut or vegetable oil

1 cinnamon stick, bruised

3 star anise

small piece fresh ginger, peeled and grated

1 Thai red chile, seeded and chopped

$1^2/_3$ cups jasmine rice

5 cups vegetable stock

3 cups small broccoli florets

2 cups trimmed and halved green beans

1 red bell pepper, seeded and chopped

1 orange bell pepper, seeded and chopped

1 cup trimmed sugar snap peas

8 baby corn

1 tbsp. freshly chopped cilantro, to garnish (optional)

Tasty tip

Other fragrant ingredients can be used if you prefer—try lemongrass, bruised green cardamom pods and ground allspice.

Spiced Tomato Pilaf

1. Wash the rice in several changes of water until the water remains relatively clear. Drain the rice and cover with fresh water. Let soak for 30 minutes. Drain well and set aside.

2. Heat the wok, then melt the butter and add the cardamoms, star anise, cloves, black peppercorns, and the cinnamon stick. Cook gently for 30 seconds. Increase the heat and add the onion. Stir-fry for 7–8 minutes until tender and starting to brown. Add the drained rice and cook for an additional 2–3 minutes.

3. Strain the tomatoes and mix with sufficient warm water to make 2 cups. Pour this into the wok, season to taste with salt and pepper, and bring to a boil.

4. Cover, reduce the heat to very low, and cook for 10 minutes. Remove the wok from the heat and leave covered for an additional 10 minutes. Do not lift the lid during cooking or resting. Finally, uncover and mix well with a fork, heat for 1 minute, then garnish with the sprigs of fresh cilantro and serve immediately.

Ingredients   SERVES 2–3

1 cup basmati rice
3 tbsp. unsalted butter
4 green cardamom pods
2 star anise
4 whole cloves
10 black peppercorns
2-in. piece cinnamon stick
1 large red onion, peeled and
  finely sliced
6 oz. canned chopped tomatoes
salt and freshly ground black pepper
fresh cilantro sprigs, to garnish

Food fact

Star anise is native to southwest China and comes from a small evergreen tree. The spice is actually the fruit of the tree and is harvested just before ripening. It is used extensively in oriental and Indian cuisine, imparting an aromatic anise flavor. It is also used in herbal remedies for coughs and colds, rheumatism, and as an aid to digestion.

Bean & Cashew Stir-Fry

1 Heat a wok or large skillet, add the oil, and, when hot, add the onion and celery, and stir-fry gently for 3–4 minutes until softened.

2 Add the ginger, garlic, and chile to the wok, and stir-fry for 30 seconds. Stir in the green beans, snow peas, and cashews, and continue to stir-fry for 1–2 minutes until the nuts are golden brown.

3 Dissolve the sugar in the stock, then blend with the sherry, soy sauce, and vinegar. Stir into the bean mixture and bring to a boil. Simmer gently, stirring occasionally, for 3–4 minutes until the beans and snow peas are tender but still crisp, and the sauce has thickened slightly. Season to taste with salt and pepper. Transfer to a warmed serving bowl, or spoon onto individual plates. Sprinkle with freshly chopped cilantro and serve immediately.

Ingredients　　SERVES 4

3 tbsp. sunflower oil
1 onion, peeled and finely chopped
1 celery stalk, trimmed and chopped
1-in. piece ginger, peeled and grated
2 garlic cloves, peeled and crushed
1 red chile, seeded and
　finely chopped
1 cup trimmed and halved
　green beans
$1^1/_4$ cups diagonally sliced (into
　thirds) snow peas
$2^1/_3$ cups unsalted cashews
1 tsp. brown sugar
$^1/_2$ cup vegetable stock
2 tbsp. dry sherry
1 tbsp. light soy sauce
1 tsp. red wine vinegar
salt and freshly ground black pepper
freshly chopped cilantro, to garnish

Zucchini & Tarragon Tortilla

1 Peel the potatoes and slice thinly. Dry the slices in a clean dish towel to get them as dry as possible. Heat the oil in a large, heavy skillet, add the onion, and cook for 3 minutes. Add the potatoes along with a little salt and pepper, then stir the potatoes and onion lightly to coat in the oil.

2 Reduce the heat to the lowest possible setting, cover, and cook gently for 5 minutes. Turn the potatoes and onion over and continue to cook for an additional 5 minutes. Give the pan a shake every now and again to ensure that the potatoes do not stick to the bottom or burn. Add the zucchini, then cover and cook for an additional 10 minutes.

3 Beat the eggs and tarragon together and season to taste with salt and pepper. Pour the egg mixture over the vegetables and return to the heat. Cook on a low heat for up to 20–25 minutes until there is no liquid egg left on the surface of the tortilla.

4 Turn the tortilla over by inverting the pan onto the lid or a large, flat plate. Slide the tortilla back into the pan. Return the pan to the heat and cook for a final 3–5 minutes until the underside is golden brown. If preferred, place the tortilla under a preheated broiler for 4 minutes, or until set and golden brown on top. Cut into small squares and serve hot or cold with tomato wedges.

Ingredients
SERVES 4

1½ lbs. potatoes
3 tbsp. olive oil
1 onion, peeled and thinly sliced
salt and freshly ground black pepper
1 zucchini, trimmed and thinly sliced
6 large eggs
2 tbsp. freshly chopped tarragon
tomato wedges, to serve

Food fact

Almost regarded as the national dish of Spain, the tortilla is a substantial omelet traditionally made from eggs, potatoes, and onions. Here, zucchini and tarragon are added for extra flavor and color. Use even-sized, waxy potatoes, which do not break up during cooking.

Red Beet Risotto

1 Heat half the oil in a large, heavy skillet. Add the onion, garlic, thyme, and lemon zest. Cook for 5 minutes, stirring frequently, until the onion is soft and transparent, but not browned. Add the rice and stir until it is well coated in the oil.

2 Add the wine, then bring to a boil and boil rapidly until the wine has almost evaporated. Reduce the heat.

3 Keeping the pan over low heat, add a ladleful of the hot stock to the rice and cook, stirring continuously, until the stock is absorbed. Continue gradually adding the stock in this way until the rice is tender; this should take about 20 minutes. You may not need all the stock.

4 Stir in the cream, chopped beet, parsley, and half the grated Parmesan cheese. Season to taste with salt and pepper. Garnish with sprigs of fresh thyme and serve immediately with the remaining grated Parmesan cheese.

Ingredients   SERVES 6

6 tbsp. extra virgin olive oil
1 onion, peeled and finely chopped
2 garlic cloves, peeled and
    finely chopped
2 tsp. freshly chopped thyme
1 tsp. grated lemon zest
2 cups Arborio rice
$^2/_3$ cup dry white wine
$3^3/_4$ cups heated vegetable stock
2 tbsp. heavy cream
$1^1/_2$ cups peeled and finely chopped
    cooked beet
2 tbsp. freshly chopped parsley
$^3/_4$ cup freshly grated
    Parmesan cheese
salt and freshly ground black pepper
fresh thyme sprigs, to garnish

Vegetable Biryani

1 Preheat the oven to 400°F. Put 1 tablespoon of the vegetable oil in a large bowl with the onions and toss to coat. Lightly brush or spray a nonstick baking sheet with a little more oil. Spread half the onions on the baking sheet and cook on the top rack of the preheated oven for 25–30 minutes, stirring regularly, until golden and crisp. Remove from the oven and set aside for the garnish.

2 Meanwhile, heat a large, flameproof casserole dish over medium heat and add the remaining oil and onions. Cook for 5–7 minutes until softened and starting to brown. Add a little water if they start to stick. Add the garlic and ginger and cook for another minute, then add the carrot, parsnip, and sweet potato. Cook the vegetables for an additional 5 minutes. Add the curry paste and stir for a minute until everything is coated, then stir in the rice and tomatoes. After 2 minutes, add the stock and stir well. Bring to a boil, cover, and simmer over very gentle heat for about 10 minutes.

3 Add the cauliflower and peas and cook for 8–10 minutes until the rice is tender. Season to taste with salt and pepper. Serve garnished with the crispy onions, cashew nuts, raisins, and cilantro.

Ingredients SERVES 4

2 tbsp. vegetable oil, plus a little extra for brushing

2 large onions, peeled and thinly sliced lengthwise

2 garlic cloves, peeled and finely chopped

1-in. piece fresh ginger, peeled and finely grated

1 small carrot, peeled and cut into sticks

1 small parsnip, peeled and diced

1 small sweet potato, peeled and diced

1 tbsp. medium curry paste

1 cup basmati rice

4 ripe tomatoes, peeled, seeded, and diced

2$\frac{1}{2}$ cups vegetable stock

2 cups cauliflower florets

$\frac{1}{2}$ cup defrosted or fresh peas

salt and freshly ground black pepper

To garnish:

roasted cashew nuts

raisins

fresh cilantro leaves

Brown Rice Spiced Pilaf

1 Preheat the oven to 400°F. Heat the oil in a large, flameproof casserole dish and add the almonds. Cook for 1–2 minutes until just browning. Be very careful, as the nuts will burn easily.

2 Add the onion and carrot. Cook for 5 minutes until softened and starting to turn brown. Add the mushrooms and cook for an additional 5 minutes, stirring often.

3 Add the cinnamon and pepper flakes and cook for about 30 seconds before adding the apricots, currants, orange zest, and rice.

4 Stir together well and add the stock. Bring to a boil, cover tightly, and transfer to the preheated oven. Cook for 45 minutes until the rice and vegetables are tender.

5 Stir the cilantro and chives into the pilaf and season to taste with salt and pepper. Garnish with the extra chives and serve immediately.

Ingredients   SERVES 4

1 tbsp. vegetable oil
1 tbsp. blanched almonds, slivered
   or chopped
1 onion, peeled and chopped
1 carrot, peeled and diced
2 cups thickly sliced flat mushrooms
$1/4$ tsp. ground cinnamon
large pinch dried pepper flakes
$1/2$ cup coarsely chopped
   dried apricots
2 tbsp. currants
1 tbsp. orange zest
$1^{1}/_{2}$ cups brown basmati rice
$3^{3}/_{4}$ cups vegetable stock
2 tbsp. freshly chopped cilantro
2 tbsp. freshly cut chives, plus extra
   to garnish
salt and freshly ground black pepper

Food fact

Brown basmati rice is one of the healthiest rices. It slowly releases carbohydrate into the blood, thereby maintaining the body's energy levels.

Pumpkin & Chickpea Curry

1 Heat 1 tablespoon of the oil in a saucepan and add the onion. Cook gently for 5 minutes until softened.

2 Add the garlic, ginger, and spices, and cook for an additional minute. Add the chopped tomatoes and chiles and cook for another minute.

3 Add the pumpkin and curry paste and cook for 3–4 minutes before adding the stock. Stir well, bring to a boil, and simmer for 20 minutes until the pumpkin is tender.

4 Thickly slice the banana and add to the pumpkin along with the chickpeas. Simmer for an additional 5 minutes.

5 Season to taste with salt and pepper and add the chopped cilantro. Serve immediately, garnished with cilantro sprigs and some rice or naan.

Ingredients SERVES 4

1 tbsp. vegetable oil
1 small onion, peeled and sliced
2 garlic cloves, peeled and
    finely chopped
1-in. piece ginger, peeled and grated
1 tsp. ground coriander
$\frac{1}{2}$ tsp. ground cumin
$\frac{1}{2}$ tsp. ground turmeric
$\frac{1}{4}$ tsp. ground cinnamon
2 tomatoes, chopped
2 red Thai chiles, seeded
    and finely chopped
$2\frac{1}{2}$ cups cubed pumpkin or
    butternut squash flesh
1 tbsp. hot curry paste
$1\frac{1}{4}$ cups vegetable stock
1 large, firm banana
14 oz. canned chickpeas, drained
    and rinsed
salt and freshly ground black pepper
1 tbsp. freshly chopped cilantro
fresh cilantro sprigs, to garnish
rice or naan, to serve

Peperonata

1 Prepare the bell peppers by halving them lengthwise and removing the stems, seeds, and membranes, then cutting them lengthwise into strips about $1/2$ inch wide.

2 Peel the potatoes and cut into rough dice, about $1-1\frac{1}{4}$ inches across. Cut the onion lengthwise into 8 wedges.

3 Heat the olive oil in a large saucepan over medium heat. Add the onion and cook for about 5 minutes until starting to brown.

4 Add the bell peppers, potatoes, tomatoes, zucchini, ripe olives, and about 4 torn basil leaves. Season to taste with salt and pepper. Stir the mixture, cover, and cook over very low heat for about 40 minutes until the vegetables are tender but still hold their shape.

5 Transfer to a serving bowl, garnish with the remaining basil, and serve immediately with chunks of crusty bread.

Ingredients　　SERVES 4–6

2 red bell peppers
2 yellow bell peppers
1 lb. waxy potatoes
1 large onion
2 tbsp. good-quality virgin olive oil
$2\frac{1}{4}$ cups peeled, seeded, and
　chopped tomatoes ($1\frac{1}{2}$ lb.)
2 small zucchini
5 tbsp. pitted and quartered
　ripe olives
small handful basil leaves
salt and freshly ground black pepper
crusty bread, to serve

Tasty tip

Try serving with Parmesan melba toasts. To make, remove the crusts from 4 slices thin white bread. Lightly toast and allow to cool before splitting each in half by slicing horizontally. Cut into triangles, place under a broiler and toast each side for a few minutes until golden. Sprinkle with finely grated Parmesan and melt under the broiler.

Light Ratatouille

1   Seed the pepper, remove the membrane with a small, sharp knife, and dice. Thickly slice the zucchini and dice the eggplant. Slice the onion into rings.

2   Cut crosses in the tops of the tomatoes and place them in boiling water until their skins begin to peel away. Remove their skins, cut into quarters, and remove the seeds.

3   Place all the vegetables in a saucepan with the tomato juice and basil. Season to taste with salt and pepper. Bring to a boil, cover, and simmer for 15 minutes, or until the vegetables are tender. Remove the vegetables with a slotted spoon and arrange in a serving dish.

4   Bring the liquid in the saucepan to a boil and boil for 20 seconds, or until it is slightly thickened. Season the sauce to taste with salt and pepper. Pass the sauce through a strainer to remove some of the seeds and pour over the vegetables. Serve the ratatouille hot or cold.

Ingredients   SERVES 4

1 red bell pepper
2 zucchini, trimmed
1 small eggplant, trimmed
1 onion, peeled
2 ripe tomatoes
$1^1/_2$ cups wiped and halved (or quartered) button mushrooms
$^3/_4$ cup tomato juice
1 tbsp. freshly chopped basil
salt and freshly ground black pepper

Tasty tip

This dish would be perfect served as an accompaniment to any of the fish dishes in this book. It is also delicious in an omelet or as a baked-potato filling.

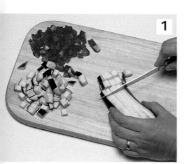

Creamy Vegetable Korma

1 Heat the ghee or oil in a large saucepan. Add the onion and cook for 5 minutes. Stir in the garlic and ginger and cook for an additional 5 minutes, or until soft and just beginning to brown.

2 Stir in the cardamom, coriander, cumin, and turmeric. Continue cooking over low heat for 1 minute, stirring.

3 Stir in the lemon zest and juice and almonds. Blend in the vegetable stock. Slowly bring to a boil, stirring occasionally.

4 Add the potatoes and vegetables. Bring back to a boil, then reduce the heat, cover, and simmer for 35–40 minutes until the vegetables are just tender. Check after 25 minutes and add more stock if needed.

5 Slowly stir in the cream and chopped cilantro. Season to taste with salt and pepper. Cook very gently until heated through, but do not boil. Serve immediately with naan.

Ingredients   SERVES 4–6

2 tbsp. ghee or vegetable oil
1 large onion, peeled and chopped
2 garlic cloves, peeled and crushed
1-in. piece fresh ginger, peeled
    and grated
4 green cardamom pods
2 tsp. ground coriander
1 tsp. ground cumin
1 tsp. ground turmeric
finely grated zest and juice of
    $1/_2$ lemon
$1/_2$ cup ground almonds
$1^3/_4$ cups vegetable stock
$2^2/_3$ cups peeled and
    diced potatoes
1 lb. mixed vegetables, such as
    cauliflower, carrots, baby corn,
    and turnips, cut into chunks
    if large
$2/_3$ cup heavy cream
3 tbsp. freshly chopped cilantro
salt and freshly ground black pepper
naan, to serve

Parsnip Tatin

1 Preheat the oven to 400°F. Sift the flour and salt into a large bowl. Add the fats and mix lightly. Using the fingertips, rub into the flour until the mixture resembles bread crumbs.

2 Sprinkle 1 tablespoon cold water into the mixture and, with a knife, start bringing the dough together. (It may be necessary to use the hands for the final stage.) If the dough does not form a ball instantly, add a little more water. Put the pastry dough in a plastic bag and chill for at least 30 minutes.

3 Heat the butter in an 8-inch skillet. Add the parsnips, arranging the cut side down, with the narrow ends of the parsnips toward the center.

4 Sprinkle the parsnips with sugar and cook for 15 minutes, turning halfway through, until golden. Add the apple juice and bring to a boil. Remove the skillet from the heat.

5 On a lightly floured surface, roll the pastry out to a size slightly larger than the skillet. Position the pastry over the parsnips and press down slightly to enclose the parsnips.

6 Bake in the preheated oven for 20–25 minutes until the parsnips and pastry are golden. Invert a warmed serving plate over the pan and carefully turn the pan over to flip the tart onto the plate. Serve immediately.

Ingredients   SERVES 4

For the flaky pastry:

1 cup all-purpose flour

pinch salt

2 tbsp. lard or shortening, cut into small cubes

3 tbsp. butter or margarine, cut into small cubes

For the filling:

4 tbsp. butter

8 small parsnips, peeled and halved

1 tbsp. brown sugar

6 tbsp. apple juice

Tasty tip

This dish is delicious served warm with a Greek salad. Feta cheese is one of the main ingredients in Greek salad and, because of its salty taste, it tastes particularly good with the creamy flavor of parsnips in this recipe.

Vegetable Cassoulet

1 Preheat the oven to 375°F. Heat 1 tablespoon of the oil in a flameproof casserole dish and add the garlic, onions, carrots, celery, and red bell pepper. Cook gently for 10–12 minutes until tender and starting to brown.

2 Add a little water if the vegetables start to stick. Add the mushrooms and cook for an additional 5 minutes until softened. Add the herbs and stir briefly.

3 Stir in the red wine and boil rapidly for about 5 minutes until reduced and syrupy. Stir in the navy beans, tomato paste, and soy sauce. Season to taste with salt and pepper.

4 Mix together the bread crumbs and parsley with the remaining tablespoon of oil. Sprinkle this mixture evenly over the top of the stew. Cover loosely with foil and transfer to the preheated oven. Cook for 30 minutes.

5 Carefully remove the foil and cook for an additional 15–20 minutes until the topping is crisp and golden. Garnish with basil sprigs and serve immediately.

Ingredients   SERVES 6

2 tbsp. olive oil
2 garlic cloves, peeled and chopped
9 pearl onions, peeled and halved
2 carrots, peeled and diced
2 celery stalks, trimmed and
    finely chopped
1 red bell pepper, seeded
    and chopped
1^1/$_2$ cups mixed mushrooms, sliced
1 tbsp. each freshly chopped
    rosemary, thyme, and sage
^{2}/$_3$ cup red wine
14 oz. canned navy beans
4 tbsp. tomato paste
1 tbsp. dark soy sauce
salt and freshly ground black pepper
^{1}/$_2$ cup fresh bread crumbs
1 tbsp. freshly chopped parsley
basil sprigs, to garnish

Thai Noodles & Vegetables with Tofu

1 Drain the tofu well and cut into cubes. Put into a shallow dish with the soy sauce and lime zest. Stir well to coat and leave to marinate for 30 minutes.

2 Meanwhile, put the lemongrass and chile on a cutting board and bruise with the side of a large knife, ensuring the blade is pointing away from your body. Put the vegetable stock in a large saucepan and add the lemongrass, chile, ginger, garlic, and cilantro. Bring to a boil, cover, and simmer gently for 20 minutes.

3 Strain the stock into a clean saucepan. Return to a boil and add the noodles, tofu and its marinade, and the mushrooms. Simmer gently for 4 minutes.

4 Add the carrots, snow peas, bok choy, and cilantro, and simmer for an additional 3–4 minutes until the vegetables are just tender. Season to taste with salt and pepper. Garnish with cilantro sprigs and serve immediately.

Ingredients SERVES 4

$1/_4$ lb. firm tofu
2 tbsp. soy sauce
2 tsp. grated lime zest
2 lemongrass stalks
1 red chile
4 cups vegetable stock
2 slices fresh ginger, peeled
2 garlic cloves, peeled
2 fresh cilantro sprigs
$2^1/_2$ cups dried egg noodles
$1^3/_4$ cups shiitake or button
    mushrooms, sliced if large
2 carrots, peeled and cut
    into matchsticks
1 cup snow peas
$2^1/_2$ cups bok choy or other
    Chinese cabbage
1 tbsp. freshly chopped cilantro
salt and freshly ground black pepper
fresh cilantro sprigs, to garnish

Pad Thai Noodles with Mushrooms

1 Fill a wok or large skillet with water, and bring to a boil. Turn off the heat, gently drop in the noodles and leave for 3–4 minutes or according to package directions. Drain well and set aside.

2 Dry the wok or skillet and heat. Add the oil and garlic and fry until just golden. Add the egg and stir quickly to break it up. Cook for a few seconds before adding the noodles and mushrooms. Scrape down the sides of the pan to ensure they mix with the egg and garlic.

3 Add the lemon juice, fish sauce, sugar, cayenne pepper, scallions, and half the bean sprouts, stirring quickly all the time. Cook over high heat for an additional 2–3 minutes until everything is heated through.

4 Turn on to a serving plate. Sprinkle with the remaining bean sprouts. Garnish with the chopped peanuts and cilantro and serve immediately.

Ingredients SERVES 4

2 cups flat rice noodles or rice vermicelli
1 tbsp. vegetable oil
2 garlic cloves, peeled and finely chopped
1 large egg, lightly beaten
2 cups mixed mushrooms, such as shiitake, oyster, field, brown, and wild mushrooms
2 tbsp. lemon juice
$1\frac{1}{2}$ tbsp. Thai fish sauce
$\frac{1}{2}$ tsp. sugar
$\frac{1}{2}$ tsp. cayenne pepper
2 scallions, trimmed and cut into 1-in. pieces
$\frac{1}{4}$ cup fresh bean sprouts

To garnish:
chopped roasted peanuts
freshly chopped cilantro

Rice Nuggets in Herby Tomato Sauce

1 Pour the stock into a large saucepan. Add the bay leaf. Bring to a boil, add the rice, stir, then cover and simmer for 15 minutes. Uncover, reduce the heat to low, and cook for an additional 5 minutes until the rice is tender and all the stock is absorbed, stirring often toward the end of the cooking time. Remove from the heat and let cool.

2 Stir the cheese, egg yolk, flour, and parsley into the rice. Season to taste, then shape into 20 walnut-size balls. Cover and refrigerate.

3 To make the sauce, heat the oil in the cleaned saucepan and cook the onion for 5 minutes. Add the garlic and bell pepper and cook for an additional 5 minutes until soft. Stir in the chopped tomatoes and simmer gently for 3 minutes. Stir in the chopped basil and season to taste.

4 Add the rice nuggets to the sauce and simmer for an additional 10 minutes, or until the rice nuggets are cooked through and the sauce has reduced a little. Spoon onto serving plates and serve hot, sprinkled with Parmesan cheese.

Ingredients   SERVES 4

$2^{1}/_{2}$ cups vegetable stock
1 bay leaf
1 cup risotto rice
$^{1}/_{2}$ cup shredded cheddar cheese
1 large egg yolk
1 tbsp. all-purpose flour
2 tbsp. freshly chopped parsley
salt and freshly ground black pepper
grated Parmesan cheese, to serve

For the herby tomato sauce:

1 tbsp. olive oil
1 onion, peeled and thinly sliced
1 garlic clove, peeled and crushed
1 small yellow bell pepper, seeded and diced
14 oz. canned chopped tomatoes
1 tbsp. freshly chopped basil

Helpful hint

It is important that the stock is absorbed completely by the rice nuggets. Stir all the time for the last minute of cooking to prevent the rice from sticking.

Red Lentil Kedgeree with Avocado & Tomatoes

1 Put the rice and lentils in a strainer and rinse under cold running water. Tip into a bowl, then pour over enough cold water to cover and leave to soak for 10 minutes.

2 Heat the butter and oil in a saucepan. Add the chopped onion and cook gently, stirring occasionally, for 10 minutes until softened. Stir in the cumin, cardamom pods and bay leaf and cook for another minute, stirring all the time.

3 Drain the rice and lentils, rinse again and add to the onion in the saucepan. Stir in the vegetable stock and bring to a boil. Reduce the heat, cover the saucepan and simmer for 14–15 minutes until the rice and lentils are tender.

4 Meanwhile, place the diced avocado in a bowl and toss with the lemon juice. Stir in the tomatoes and chopped cilantro. Season to taste with salt and pepper.

5 Once the rice is cooked, fluff it up with a fork, spoon into a warmed serving dish and spoon the avocado mixture on top. Garnish with lemon or lime slices and serve.

Ingredients   SERVES 4

heaping ³/₄ cup basmati rice
³/₄ cup red lentils
1 tbsp. butter
1 tbsp. sunflower oil
1 medium onion, peeled and chopped
1 tsp. ground cumin
4 green cardamom pods, bruised
1 bay leaf
2 cups vegetable or chicken stock
1 ripe avocado, peeled, pitted,
    and diced
1 tbsp. lemon juice
4 plum tomatoes, peeled and diced
2 tbsp. freshly chopped cilantro
salt and freshly ground black pepper
lemon or lime slices, to garnish

Tasty tip

Although basmati rice and red lentils do not need to be presoaked, it improves the results in this recipe: the rice will have very light, fluffy, separate grains, and the lentils will just begin to break down, giving a creamier texture.

Index